THE COTSWOLD CANALS WALK

(Stroudwater and Thames and Severn)

The Stroudwater and Thames and Severn Canals traverse some of the most beautiful parts of the English countryside, rich in mills and flowing water for the once prosperous woollen industry.

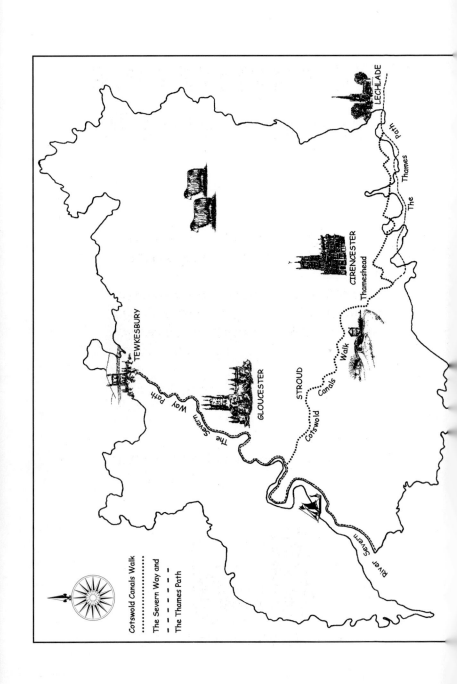

Cotswold Canals Walk

The Severn Way and

The Thames Path

LECHLADE

The Thames Path

The Thames

CIRENCESTER

Thameshead

TEWKESBURY

GLOUCESTER

STROUD

The Severn Way Path

Cotswold

Canals

Walk

River Severn

THE COTSWOLD CANALS WALK

(Stroudwater and Thames and Severn)

> When you join the Thames and Severn Canal
> at Stroud, it is but twenty- eight miles and a
> few odd furlongs before you come to
> Inglesham, where the water of the canal joins
> the Isis and all signs of the tow-path are lost to
> you for ever. But those twenty-eight miles are
> worth a thousand for the wealth of their colour
> alone.
>
> *The Flower of Gloucester*
> T. Temple Thurston

Designed and compiled by Gerry Stewart
Illustrations by Genny Proctor

COUNTRYSIDE MATTERS

Published in 2000 by
COUNTRYSIDE MATTERS
15 Orchard Road
Alderton
Tewkesbury
Gloucestershire   GL20 8NS
www.countryside-matters.co.uk

Typeset by Ex Libris Press
Bradford on Avon, Wiltshire

Printed and bound by Cromwell Press
Trowbridge, Wiltshire

ISBN 09527870 3 2

Contents

Credits

The Publishers wish to express their grateful thanks for the use of the following poems which enhance the Cotswold Canals Walk. While efforts have been made to contact copyright holders it is, despite modern technology, amazingly difficult to track people down. The publishers would therefore be pleased to hear from anyone whom they have not been able to contact.

Roger Davison, for 'Barges at Purton', from *Five Particular Places*, The Pear Tree Press. U.A. Fanthorpe and the Peterloo Poets for 'On buying Sheet 163' from *Standing To*, Samuel French Ltd. as Literary Representative of John Drinkwater for 'Legacy' from *Tides*. Orion Publishing Group for 'Near Oldbury Sands' by Brian Waters, from *The Bristol Channel* (Dent 1955). Phoenix House Press, for 'Gloucestershire Exile', from *Cotswold Lad* by Sid Knight. Sheila Simmonds, for 'Stroudwater Shades'. Alan Sutton Publishing Ltd., for extracts from *Notes and Recollections of Stroud* by Paul Hawkins Fisher.

My grateful thanks are also due to The Windrush Press, publishers of *Forest and Vale and High Blue Hill* and *Between the Severn and Wye*, both compiled by Johnny Coppin and where I first read some of these poets work.

Acknowledgments

My thanks to my daughter, Genevieve Proctor, who spent a good deal of time, in the middle of moving and settling into a new house, producing the illustrations which enhance the Cotswold Canals Walk.

My wife Kate, although not required to shuttle cars across wintry hills on this occasion, has walked with me on most field trips gathering snippets of useful information, making helpful comments and, where necessary providing criticism. In particular her patient proof reading has removed the majority of my errors and omissions

Mr George Gilbody, stalwart that he is, was kind enough to physically check my route description against the reality on the ground. Although he undertook the project partly as exercise and therapy after a nasty ankle fracture I know that considerable effort was needed by him. It was a valiant effort for which I am very grateful.

Finally, preservation of the canals is in the hands of the Cotswold Canals Trust, being the successor to the earlier Stroudwater Canal Society, which has the long term objective of restoration and operation of both canals.

Apart from the preservation and restoration achieved to date, which has served to bring this splendid amenity to public notice, the Trust has contributed significantly to the national debate on the future of inland waterways.

Author's Note

The Cotswold Canals Walk is predominantly along public footpaths and bridleways, but in a few places roads have to be used. These are mostly back roads and lanes and even in an age of mass car ownership, are comparatively quiet.

The sketch maps are quite adequate for the walk, but to relate to the surrounding country side OS Landranger 162 & 163, or for greater detail Outdoor Leisure 14 and Explorer Maps 168, 169 and 170, are necessary.

Public transport is helpful for linear walks in the Stroud Valleys and to the villages between Cirencester and Swindon, but is more difficult to co-ordinate across the upper reaches between Sapperton and Lechlade. Mini buses or taxis, hired according to the size of the party, offer an economic way to the start or finish of sections.

Whilst care has been taken to ensure that the information provided in this book is accurate, neither the author nor publisher can accept responsibility for any errors or omissions or for the interpretation of the information by users of this guide book.

This is not a guide to the canals or even primarily about them and canal enthusiasts must look elsewhere to the many publications available for their enthusiasm.

I have gleaned a good deal of information from 'The Stroudwater and Thames & Severn Canals Towpath Guide' by Handford and Viner, but this is considerably out of date now.

This description is for walkers, many of whom, in my experience, enjoy a theme or added interests in their walks. Following the route of an old canal - sometimes directly on a towpath but elsewhere along nearby fieldpaths and bridleways, provides the necessary motif.

The facility to walk through the landscape of the Stroud and

AUTHOR'S NOTE

Golden Valleys, redolent of industrial and archaeological antiquity, is a pleasurable and rewarding experience. The journey on foot passing historic industries and workplaces in close conjunction with the differing eras of turnpike, rail, river and canal, providing a vivid contrast.

I have included towpaths wherever they are open for public use even though this may only be permissive in places, otherwise where the towpath is inaccessible public rights of way are utilised. It must be remembered that changes continually take place in the countryside, hedges disappear, new fences, sometimes without stiles or gates, arise and paths may be difficult to follow through crops. Also, public paths are subject to legal diversions which may not be reflected in current maps. The Highway Authority's signposting should reveal any changes but the situation may not always be clear on the ground.

Introduction

The River Severn was early a major trade route. The Romans, although probably not venturing too far up stream in their Triremes established ferry stations at Aust, Arlingham, and Gloucester, while fords at Framilode and Longney were already in use long before they came.

After them came the Saxons, and today eight out of ten Severnside names are Saxon in origin. Odda's Chapel at Deerhurst is built of stone rafted up stream from Westbury cliff, and iron and stone were ferried from the forest on the west bank, both up and down river. The Danes in turn raided up to Gloucester and settled for a time at Cirencester until they were moved on by Alfred.

King Canute is said to have ordered...'that two oaks be given to the woman who had the ferry at Newnham that she might build a boat'. By 1067 the Norman, Robert Fitzhamon, was constructing Tewkesbury Abbey with stone brought up river from his native Caen in Normandy.

River trade and commerce grew rapidly and the riverside communities became increasingly dependent for their livelihoods on waterborne traffic. Pills, where tidal streams joined the river, were natural 'harbours' where vessels could load and unload. Around these settlements had arisen and an area at each was often allocated as a parish wharf. In particular the Hock ditch at Frampton, and Framilode, Bullo and Cone Pills, became well known and each had an ensuing history.

An early record refers to a Frampton ship trading with Bristol and Ireland in 1377, and by 1831 fifty families were employed directly by Severn water traffic, while boatbuilding continued at the Pill up to 1880.

There is evidence of similar activity at almost every town, village and community on the river, from Chepstow to Tewkesbury, as over the years, vessels progressed from drags to barges and trows. The bore tides racing upstream carried vessels past Gloucester in a fraction of the time it took to work them down. Because of more favourable conditions for using sails and 'freshes' flowing downstream, vessels on the Severn relied less on towing, either by men or horses, than did the Thames or other river traffic.

The industrialisation of the Ironbridge Gorge and the east Shropshire coalfield were mainly responsible for the increasing commerce of the Severn. Certainly it led to the peak of trade on the river and also to its eventual decline. During the 17th Century, the Severn provided the coal proprietors access to a wide range of markets, and the invention of coke smelting gave added impetus though the growth of the iron trade.

The first boat load of coal had passed through Tewkesbury and Gloucester in 1570 and 200 years later this became 100,000 tons shipped annually downstream to the banks of the Severn and where it was distributed through the adjacent countryside. ....'*also great quantities of grain, bar and pig iron, earthen wares, hops, cyder and wool were exported to Bristol and other places. This traffic was carried in vessels of two sorts, the lesser kind called barges or frigates, being from 40-60 feet in length, and have a single mast and square sail, carrying from 20-40 tons. The Trows or larger vessels are from 40-80 tons burthen, and these have a main and top mast about 80 feet high, with square sails and some have mizzen masts. They are generally from 16-20 feet wide and 60 feet in length.'*

> *Beyond a row of steel pontoons*
> *where Sharpness canal reflects the sky,*
> *the river, treacherous and mild*
> *uncovers mud-flats soft as curd,*
> *moulded by the ebbing tide.*

In calmness, describing history,
and intimate as ancient ruins,
*   with picturesque tenacity*
the hulks rot, stranded shoalwise,
*   some more grassy bank than barge*
compacted in the soil which covers them.

The structure and the bulk remains,
of pitch caulked timbers
*   studded with iron,*
stout ribs retaining graceful lines
*   of bow and stern,*
cleats warped by hawsers
*   into hour-glass shapes,*
tillers jammed at awkward angles
from the moment they were beached,
like remnants from outlandish fleets
*   left here to stem the Severn's tide.*

'Barges at Purton'   Roger Davison

*   *   *   *   *   *

For centuries rivers were made navigable by flash weirs. These were primarily to provide a head of water to power corn, wool or sawmills, and the introduction of a movable section in the weir allowed a vessel to 'shoot' through with the rush of water. Moving against the flow necessitated winching through with ropes and pulleys from the bank, or otherwise waiting until the river equalised which was wasteful of water and of time in waiting for the water to back up above the weir.

Progress came in the form of a box chamber constructed in the weir, with gates at either end, enabling a boat to enter the lower level and rise to the higher as the chamber filled. The first such is attributed to the Chinese in AD 983.

Straightening or 'canalising' rivers soon followed lock improvements and began to include the construction of new channels to bypass difficult river sections. The first in Britain being the Exeter Canal in 1564/66.

Leonardi da Vinci, as with many other engineering attributes, invented the swinging or mitred gates for locks as still used on many British canals today. This was the major factor in canal building - the construction of artificial waterways from or over watersheds. In England the first was Brindley's Trent and Mersey in 1776, followed by the Leeds and Liverpool over the Pennines, the Kennet and Avon linking the Thames to the Bristol Avon, and the Firth and Clyde.

This activity produced up to 100 miles of canal in 1760, 2224 miles by 1790, 3691 miles by 1820 and 4023 miles by 1850, carrying a multitude of goods. But coal was always the predominant cargo to fuel the new age of steam and with that came the railways and the rapid decline of canals.

*   *   *   *   *   *

From earliest days, almost every stream and river with a reasonable flow was harnessed as a source of power, the vast majority powering simple corn mills. Gradually other uses were found for this relatively reliable source of power. In the Forest of Dean, water wheels were harnessed to drive the bellows of blast furnaces, work trip hammers and to pump water from mine shafts.

The Frome and its tributaries eventually powered scores of increasingly mechanised woollen cloth mills which were usually of simple construction from local materials. Later, because of the high incidence of fire in cloth mills, designs changed, such as Stanley Mill at Ryeford, built of brick on an expensive iron framework.

Over the centuries, as mills became redundant through economic down turns, they were often reused, sometimes for a succession of different purposes. In the Stroud valleys, for instance, as the woollen industry diminished the manufacture of walking sticks, hosiery knitting, engineering and, later, silk throwing, brought a new lease of life for many mills.

The Stroudwater Canal was promoted by clothiers in the Stroud valleys mainly to obtain coal more cheaply from Shropshire, Staffordshire and the Forest of Dean. It was completed in 1779 and climbed from the Severn via 12 locks in 8 miles. The locks were wide gauge to take Severn Trows up to 72 ft long and 15 1/2 beam. Still owned by the *'Company of Proprietors of the Stroudwater Navigation'*, it is the oldest privately owned canal in Europe.

The Stroudwater Navigation is significant in the development of canals and helps to dispose the historical myth that the British canal age began with the Duke of Bridgwater's canal in 1761.

The first of five attempts, before it became a reality, the Stroudwater was planned in the 1720's and is therefore one of the earliest canals to be conceived. A group of wealthy landowners engaged in the woollen trade obtained an Act of Parliament to build a waterway in an era when the 10 miles of road from the Severn to Stroud was a major obstacle for the transport of coal. For Shropshire coal, which cost 11 shillings (55p) transported to Framilode, was almost twice as much at Stroud. Disagreement with the mill owners along the Frome, who were concerned about the likely loss of water, caused the initial scheme to fail.

When Richard Cambridge settled at Whitminster House, he commenced extensive landscaping and improvements to his estate, which included making the Frome navigable from the Severn to the Bristol Road. There is no evidence that he constructed any locks and he may therefore have been the first to bypass mill weirs by using cranes to transfer goods from boat to boat.

The next attempt, was in 1754, when John Dallaway of Brimscombe, mooted a canal to local dignitaries and businessmen. Employing a Tewkesbury engineer, Thomas Chin, he planned to make the Frome navigable using pound locks and cutting new channels past every mill. Again the virulent opposition of mill owners led to this effort being abandoned.

Four Tewkesbury men, led by a John Kemmett, next proposed a canal without locks so that no obstruction of the mills, or extraction of water from the Frome, would occur. This required using cranes to transfer goods from boat to boat at each change of level. An Act of Parliament authorised the canal in 1759, and work commenced on widening and straightening the Frome and converting mill ponds into navigable channels around the mills.

Kemmett's canal probably reached Stonehouse, but the repeated handling of goods caused excessive damage and was too expensive to compete with the new turnpike roads. Although this too was abandoned in 1763, evidence of the work carried out then is still visible.

The successful completion of canals elsewhere in the country gave impetus for a final effort by a new Stroudwater Canal Company. The successful completion of a new cut from Framilode to Wallbridge then led to the conception of a canal to connect the two great rivers of England, the Thames and Severn. It was engineered by Robert Whitworth, with 42 locks and a tunnel over two miles in length in the 29 miles between Wallbridge and Inglesham.

Opened in 1789, the upper reaches of the canal were never adequately supplied with water which seriously affected the amount of trade and profitability achieved.

The section between Inglesham and Chalford was closed in 1927 and the remainder to Stroud in 1933. The Stroudwater continued to operate up to 1941 but was legally abandoned, in common with many similar waterways, in 1954.

*　　*　　*　　*　　*　　*

This situation might have remained, with further deterioration and decay, but for the setting up of the Inland Waterways Association in 1946. Their immediate and strenuous campaigning against government and public inertia was the turning point in the history of the canal network in Britain. The public taste was quickly whetted by the imaginative conception of an important national commodity being turned into a recreational amenity in a setting of well preserved industrial archaeology.

The earlier Stroudwater Canal Society became the Stroudwater, Thames and Severn Canal Trust, in 1975, the major objective being the eventual restoration and operation of both canals as a recreational amenity while preserving the interests of development, heritage and conservation.

These objectives, according to the recent announcements by both the chairman of British Waterways and the Minister for the Environment, seem likely to be realised much sooner than was probably envisaged as part of a new impetus for the reclamation of the national canal network.

One of the Trust's major aims is the promotion of the towpaths as a long distance footpath for the future. I feel that this guidebook will help to achieve that by introducing the canals to a wider audience and encouraging the spread of public interest and anticipation of future developments.

Gerry Stewart
August 2000

The Stroudwater –
Framilode to Wallbridge

On a quiet day, Upper Framilode, at the end of a cul-de-sac lane leading from Saul, seems remote from the rush of the world. The church is hidden until you arrive outside, the tower more easily seen from the river than from landward. Inside, the church is austere but friendly, and on display a copy of the original plan for the Stroudwater canal is an auspicious and welcome start for our walk.

From the flood-wall, the wide sweep of the river, once one of the busiest in Europe and alive with craft, is the story of Framilode.

It is a pity that the site of Framilode lock, where the first stone was laid on 30th May 1775, is inaccessible and the lock basin now a garden. But the lock house is still visible and the towpath, leaving the road eastwards, is a public right of way. The canal, although often covered with reeds and weed, has a good depth of water.

Almost immediately pass the Ship Inn which provided refreshment for the Trowmen after working their boats down the river. After crossing Moor Street several stiles are an unnecessary nuisance on the tow path which soon becomes the bank of the River Frome where canal and river were combined for flood control in the 1970's.

The line of the canal is still visible slightly east of the river leading to a house, shielded by trees, which was formerly the Drum and Monkey Inn on the canal side. Shortly afterwards, where the Frome ahead can be seen emerging from a culvert beneath the Gloucester - Sharpness Ship Canal, walk up to the lockside at Saul Junction where the line of the Stroudwater meets and crosses the major ship canal. A notice board relates the objects and work of the Cotswold Canals Trust in preserving the Stroudwater and Thames and Severn.

This potted history of the two canals should serve to whet the appetite for the walk as it informs that the Stroudwater and Thames and Severn canals traverse some of the most beautiful parts of the English countryside, rich in mills and flowing water for the once prosperous woollen industry.

One of the major objectives of the Canals Trust is for the towpath, or alternative nearby paths, to become a recognised long distance footpath. The towpath already links the Severn Way path along the east bank of the Severn, to the Thames Path National Trail at Thameshead, while the Cotswold Way National Trail crosses the canal at Ryeford.

Fortunately, between Framilode and Sapperton Tunnel much of the towpath is already public right of way while other lengths are accessible along permissive paths or by nearby public paths.

At the canal junction the original line of the Stroudwater was altered to accommodate the construction of the later Gloucester - Berkeley canal. The Junction lock was necessary to facilitate the change in level and from here northwards to Whitminster lock the Stroudwater was raised slightly on an embankment.

FRAMILODE TO WALLBRIDGE

The river Severn was never a safe waterway for any type of craft. The huge tidal range, one of the highest in the world, and constant bore tides resulting in ever shifting sandbanks, rock beds protruding across the channel, rapid floods and sudden winds, all combined to make the lower Severn a most difficult and dangerous stretch of navigation.

A Bill for the provision of a canal to avoid the treacherous 30 miles below Gloucester was enacted by Parliament at the height of 'Canal mania', but as with the Stroudwater, it suffered many false starts before it was commenced in 1794.

Financial and constructional difficulties delayed completion of the length from Gloucester to Saul Junction until 1820, while the lower section, subsequently changed to join the river at Sharpness instead of Berkeley, was not open until 1827.

The canal is said to be constructed to a rule of 16' being 16 miles long, 16 yards wide, 16 feet deep and having 16 bridges along its length?

> *The Brig men, studying the hourly change*
> *Of depth, of current speed, of current range,*
> *Of shoals becoming deeps; of deeps that filled*
> *(No warning given) as the river willed;*
> *Of sands engulfing any ship that struck;*
> *In depthless unplumbed squotulence of muck...*
> 'Near Oldbury Sands'   Brian Waters

Cross the Sharpness canal by the swing footbridge, and pass the Junction House to a well maintained towpath along an attractive length of the Stroudwater with moored canal longboats a feature.

From Walk Bridge, originally a wooden swing bridge, a path continues alongside the canal to the recently renovated Whitminster lock where the canal formerly joined the river. Silting problems led to separate channels being constructed, only to be combined again when land drainage work was carried out in the 1970's. The towpath passes through a copse and continues to a stile and farm bridge where a choice of route becomes available.

The river, having the appearance of the canal which Kemmet engineered over two hundred years ago, bends right though the fields to Fromebridge Mill with a pleasant route along the floodbank. Additionally, from the first bend in the river a public footpath forks across the field and follows the hedgerow. Both routes exit onto a lane leading past the mill, (there is no access to the mill), to reach the Bristol - Gloucester road. Turn left there and cross to a footpath along the right bank of the Frome.

To continue with the canal, cross the river by the bridge, where an aqueduct originally carried the canal over the river, and follow the track to rejoin the canal. This length of the Stroudwater, even with wartime pill boxes looming large, is a fine feature, wide and brim full of water with shapely willows along the far bank and mallards and swans drifting past.

Shortly cross a track from Stonepits Bridge where a footpath leads to Whitminster. *Originally a swing bridge provided access to the stone and gravel pits nearby at Frampton.* Continue on the well used towpath over a stile and passing the shapely Occupation Bridge which was provided for farm use when the canal divided the fields.

After a field gate, where the ditch crossing is sometimes very muddy, a second concrete pill box dominates the canal bank opposite the site of Bristol Road Wharf where the Wharf House, now enlarged and modernised, still stands. *The first cargo, of coal reached the Wharf from Framilode in December 1776 and because of the reasonably good road running north and south this became an important wharf for the distribution of coal.*

FRAMILODE TO WALLBRIDGE

*The Pill boxes were Second World War strong points
erected in a series of defensive arcs across southern England,
when the threat of invasion by German forces was very real.*

Cross a stile to the verge of the Gloucester - Bristol road. The
roundabout occupies the site of the original Bristol Road Bridge
and Lock and the road beyond is over the canal bed.

*From the roundabout Fromebridge Mill, now a pub/restaurant
can be visited, but note that there is no access to the lane or footpath
of the alternative route beyond the mill and you can only return to
this point. Hopefully this may change in time enabling a circular
return route to Saul and Framilode as well as giving access to the
next section of the walk to Eastington.*

*Fromebridge Mill occupies a site which was recorded at
Domesday and has been used for corn milling, malting, and
fulling. Iron and wire were produced from the 1760s and later a
brass works was added, but the mill had reverted to corn milling
about 1850 which continued until 1990.*

*Fulling - the cleaning and thickening of cloth by removing
natural grease. 'Fullers earth' is a clay compound which lathers
easily as a ' soap' with a capacity to absorb grease.*

Turn right, towards Bristol, and walk to the road bridge over the
Frome and cross to a footpath along the right hand bank of the river.
For the next mile the river follows the course created when
Kemmett cut his 'canal' through a dozen meanders. These low lying
water meadows, on either side of the motorway, are marked on old
maps as Frampton Mead and Eastington Mead.

*The Stroudwater contoured the other side of the low valley across
the river, the canal bed buried beneath the road linking to the*

motorway and Stonehouse. The red bricked Hyde Bridge, which stood isolated in the fields some twenty five years ago, is long gone.

Beyond the pleasant pastoral scene of the Frome, with swans preening on the bank beneath willow trees, the Cotswold edge appears distant and grey blue. It strains the imagination that, 200 years ago, boats sailed from Gloucester, and climbed to this skyline to reach the Thames.

The tranquil scene is frequently enhanced by buzzards, herons and ducks but not, to date, by dippers. This pleasantry is disrupted by the rush of traffic on the A 38 behind, and the increasing roar from the motorway in front. On the other side of the river a line of willows show the pronounced line of previous meanders.

After the motorway underpass Alder trees adorn the river bank with a purplish haze in February light and recently pollarded willows show yellow and green, and in weak sunlight, orange. This all serves to provide a pleasant contrast to the industrial scene of Meadow Mill on the opposite bank, now modernised and with the earlier industrial clutter now replaced by low roofed aluminium clad buildings.

Meadow Mill was built about 1811 when the River Frome was straightened and enlarged to form a wide mill pond, the building materials being transported along the Stroudwater. About 1826 steam power was installed but cloth production ended in 1906 and Leatherboard was produced up to 1935.

The Frome divides just prior to the Eastington - Stonehouse road. At the road turn left, crossing the nearer stream and then right, through one of a pair of wrought iron squeeze stiles. Another arm of the Frome flows in from the right, from Millend Mill visible through the trees a field away.

FRAMILODE TO WALLBRIDGE

Millend Mill was a fulling mill in the 15th Century and belonged to Leonard Stanley Priory. It was rebuilt about 1818 when steam power was installed for the processes of fulling, bleaching and drying. It later worked as a corn and saw mill and, by 1920 as maltings, being gutted by fire soon afterwards.

Walk up the narrow field inclining left to another squeeze stile and a footbridge over the other branch of the Frome. In the churchyard of St Michael and all Angels at Eastington bench seats, surrounded by snowdrops on our visit, await passing wayfarers. *Around the church, perhaps looking closer than I did, buttresses and headstones are said to show evidence of arrows and swords being sharpened in a previous age.*

From the lychgate at the front of the church cross the lane to further squeeze stiles and turn left along a causeway path back to the road.

Cross directly to a grass track which leads to the canalside at Chipman's Platt, a site of considerable activity 220 years ago when the canal was being cut, and of busy commerce for a considerable period afterwards. This may become a busy scene again in the future, with vessels locking up and down the Stroudwater.

To the left is the site of Westfield lock, the first of five which raised the canal to the level at Stonehouse. In the field, Westfield bridge, a later addition to the canal, shows the line of the canal back towards Whitminster Wharf.

Turn and follow the canal eastwards, past Dock lock which was renamed from Court Orchard lock when a dry dock with carpenters and blacksmiths workshops was constructed.

The Canal Company eventually repaired all its own boats at this yard, built lock gates and swing bridges, provided ironmongery for gates and a multitude of other uses, as well as storing timber, stone and bricks, even the Company ice breaker was kept here! The yard developed into one of the most important installations on the canal. The Dock House, now private, was provided for the Company's resident Engineer.

Cross the road where the original Pike Bridge once stood, the structure which replaced it in the 1920's was in turn removed to make way for the present layout. The towpath, now on the north bank, in deference to the local big wig at Eastington Park, passes the Lock House, which was previously a Toll House for the Eastington - Stonehouse Turnpike and which gave Pike Lock its name.

The canal parallels the road for a short distance, an attractive reach of the canal and the scene of some of the earliest restoration work by the Canals Trust, leading to Blunder Lock. Properly this was to have been named Nassfield Lock, but was apparently gleefully renamed Blunder by the workforce when it was realised that it had been constructed to the wrong level. This may have been a deliberate act by the engineer, Edmund Lingard, who was already under notice at the time and felt himself badly treated. Perhaps an early case of unfair dismissal by the Company?

With the re-naming of Blunder, the next Lock, originally intended to be Upper Nassfield, became plain Nassfield although commonly referred to by the boatmen as *'Top o Five'*. It has subsequently become Newtown Lock possibly in recognition of the canal settlement which grew up here?

Roving Bridge has business like proportions for the Severn Trows and, in addition to providing access to Eastington Park, it mainly served to get the hauliers, men or mules, to the towpath, now back on the south bank, without the need to stop and unhitch the tow.

The hamlet of Newtown, viewed from the bridge, is now a suburb of Stonehouse. The dwellings probably originated as quarters for employees during the construction of the canal. The larger houses being provided for craftsmen and senior staff with an encampment and basic accommodation for the navvies and their families. Three licensed premises are recorded at that time, and although one was the New Inn, the others were probably brew houses, which often became a livelihood for widows, producing a basic necessity for the navvies.

The view opens on the right, over the valley of the Frome and the line of Kemmetts canal. The bare slopes of Selsley Common are in front and the wooded edge of Frocester hill to the south. to the left, the industrial outskirts of Stonehouse appear through the willow trees on the far bank, with Haresfield Beacon, an outlying ridge of the Cotswolds looming above.

Bonds Mill is largely hidden by high fencing topped with barbed wire but, glimpsed through a gap, a porch lintel is inscribed Anno Vict. Reg. 50 - 1887, presumably commemorating the anniversary of the accession of Queen Victoria.

The bridge to Bonds Mill has been restored and a plaque proudly announces it to be the worlds first advanced composite lifting bridge. Opened in 1994 the bridge apparently won the Institute of Structural Engineers Medal for its innovative method of construction. *The watchtower is said to have been a machine gun post when wartime production at the Mill rated military security.*

The bridge is followed by a grand sweep of canal with willows along the far bank. Lower down the contour Kemmetts canal used the nearer channel of the Frome, flowing between Aspen trees. This slope reveals the position of the Stroudwater along a low spur from Chipman's Platt. Canal dredgings were disposed of down the embankment which also served to strengthen this unsupported length.

A gate, which demarcates the boundary of Railway land, leads to an underpass through the embankment of the Bristol to Birmingham line, the canal being relegated to a small culvert. Beyond the railway the canal becomes quite expansive. Called the Ocean, there was originally a boat yard here complete with a floating platform for raising boats out for repairs. It was enlarged as a wharf for building materials when the railway was being constructed and was probably envisaged as a rail and canal interchange.

Ocean Bridge, in common with others constructed along the Stroudwater, was originally a timber swing bridge, later replaced in iron.

Stonehouse Court across the canal, now a superior hotel, was designed by Sir Edward Lutyens after the original Tudor building was destroyed by fire. Next door is St Cyr's which lost part of the churchyard when the canal was cut and this stretch of the canal may be consecrated water?

Stride out, to make up for so much loitering, to Nutshell Cottage, Bridge and House. Built together about 1780, their purpose is unknown and Canal Company archives show no record of their construction or use. They present a very atmospheric scene and provide good publicity photographs in the efforts to promote the canal.

The Ship Inn once stood at the narrow crossroads adjacent to Bridgend Bridge, and the Woolpack, a short distance up Regent Street opposite, is now the only link with the early canal trade.

Stonehouse Mill is now Upper Mills, and the former swing bridge now a nondescript feature. A few yards further, on the opposite bank, the old buildings of Wicliffe College boathouse recall a bygone age with the wide bed of the canal overhung with huge willow trees. The College boating facilities were moved to the somewhat uglier boathouse than this is at Saul Junction, when the Stroudwater was abandoned.

A good towpath continues, alongside unsightly chain link fencing surrounding various industrial buildings to Skew Bridge which now carries a cycle and footway instead of the branch railway from Stonehouse to Nailsworth. The bridge provides a view of Stanley Mill on the outskirts of Kings Stanley.

Stanley Mill dates from 1812 and was one of the first fireproof cloth mills in the country, built of brick on a skeleton of iron arches interlinked throughout its five stories. Power was provided, in turn, by water wheels, turbines and steam. The mill was run in conjunction with Ebley Mill between 1883 and 1920 and various types of cloth continued to be produced up to 1990.

On the approach to Ryeford Bridge the canal presents an attractive scene even without full restoration. The building on the opposite bank, built of Cotswold stone, is the former Anchor Inn. In front was Ryeford wharf, said to have been the largest on the canal in its hey day, with a boat building yard and slipway alongside.

The double arch of Ryeford Bridge caters for both the canal and a branch of the Frome, and is crossed by Cotswold Way Long Distance Footpath.

The Cotswold Way National Trail crosses the low ground between Doverow Hill to the north of Stonehouse and Pen Hill to the south, on its 100 mile journey from Chipping Campden to Bath.

THE COTSWOLDS CANAL WALK

On the right of the towpath the buildings belong to Ryeford sawmills and a little further on is Ryeford swing footbridge giving access to cottages which were formerly occupied by canal employees. The towpath, passing beneath alder, hazel and ash trees, narrowing to an isthmus between river and canal, both brimful and active with swans, coots, moorhens, mallards and song birds on a sunny morning.

> *Once, vessels plied these muddy waters,*
> *coal and salt and bricks their load,*
> *'Betsy', 'Perseverance', and 'Good Intent'*
> *from Bullo Pill to Framilode.*
>
> *Then, horses trod the fronded towpath*
> *flanked by meadows lush and bright,*
> *and, cumbered down, the barges followed,*
> *'Rapid', 'Endeavour', 'Guide me Right'.*
>
> *Now, weeds and rushes clog the channel,*
> *the lonely heron fishes free*
> *unmoved by shades of long-gone vessels,*
> *'Valiant', 'Rocket', 'Industry'.*
>
> 'Stroudwater Shades'   Sheila Simmonds

The path widens to an open area leading to Ryeford double lock, unique along the Stroudwater, Thames and Severn system, and the lock cottage which is similar in design to those at Framilode, Whitminster, and Chipman's Platt. From the top lock there are wide views of the surrounding hills from Kings Stanley to the south, Selsley Common above the unusual church tower, and nearer at hand, Maiden Hill to the north above Randwick.

Still silted and derelict, the next section passes through an over-grown area with potential as pleasant open public space in future.

The next mile or so of canal has been infilled but a good towpath remains with plenty of passing interest. Shortly, opposite is the site of Ebley sawmills, and the building end on to the canal was the company warehouse, part being later used as canal stables. Next to it was the site of Ebley wharf and the Bell Inn, now houses and gardens, followed by Oil Mills Bridge and the site of Oil Mills.

> *Built by Stroud mercer William Adderly in 1721 for the production of rape seed and linseed oils. In 1764 it was a fulling mill, but by 1840 a corn mill, powered by two water wheels. Two steam engines were later added driving eight pairs of mill stones. In 1909 an abortive attempt was made to generate hydro-electric power from the Frome.*
> *Mercer - a cloth merchant.*

The canal is just a memory past the extensive building, once Ebley Cloth Mills, now shared by light industry and the headquarters of Stroud District Council. Although the canal bed is beneath the car park, the restoration is an excellent revival of the otherwise derelict mill building.

> *The site of early corn and fulling mills, the present Mill structure is mainly the result of rebuilding in the 1820's when a large new mill pond was constructed to feed five water wheels. From the 1830's it was owned by the Marling family together with Stanley Mill but finally went out of use in the 1960's.*

From the car park a pleasant open space continues alongside the Frome, which could accommodate a resurrected canal in the future.

A concrete footbridge marks the open canal again where it drains into the Frome. The towpath is spacious but the waterway narrow between wide banks and householders on the opposite side seem to be encroaching.

From the present version of Hilly Orchard footbridge the canal runs straight for a short distance past recently built canal side cottages which back on to the canal edge.

The towpath rises sharply to Dudbridge, where a new road bridge has replaced the original. The two locks were originally called Franklin's, then Upper and Lower. The latter is now Dudbridge Lock and a hundred yards further on Upper is now Foundry Lock where the Victoria Inn stood alongside it. The small stream running into the canal from the north bank once powered a corn mill before flowing beneath the canal.

Many of the old wharfside buildings around Dudbridge have disappeared, with modern industries occupying some of the sites, including Dudbridge Mill.

In use since the 12th century for corn, fulling, gig and cloth milling, it developed into one of the most successful cloth mills in the district, being awarded a gold medal at the 1851 Crystal Palace Exhibition. Cloth was produced in large quantities for military and naval purposes during the first world war.

Although barely ten feet wide this stretch of canal is deep clear water, with small trees edging the banks. A row of large willow trees set back from the far bank and an avenue of regularly spaced sycamore trees create a park like setting to the canal.

The towpath widens outside modern business premises which were previously the home of Stroud Gas Works, accessed by a swing bridge across the canal. Just past the bridge the house opposite was originally two cottages at Dudbridge coal wharf, the coal being stacked on the area of the lawn. Further along, new houses standing back from the bank, are on the site of Lodgemoor Mill Pond. The houses bear slight resemblance, although larger, to original canal cottages a few yards further on beside the towpath.

From the next bridge the towpath continues ahead but an interesting diversion follows a public right of way into the mill premises. Take the first turning right past the canal cottages, which have small warehouses and stables at either end, and walk past the millpond to Fromehall Mill.

Fromehall Mill was called Brownings Mill in 1608, and was used for both fulling and corn milling. For much of its later life the mill was worked in conjunction with the Lodgemore Mill by Strachan and Company.

Retrace to the entrance and turn right, crossing the Frome by a formal stone bridge, and walk up a paved track, once used by pack ponies carrying panniers of wool and cloth, climbing behind Lodgemoor Mill. The track joins Fromehall lane before emerging on to the Bath road out of Stroud. Directly opposite, the Clothiers Arms may be a useful refreshment stop.

Lodgemore Mill originally consisted of two separate fulling mills powered by the combined waters of the Frome and the Painswick stream. It suffered the fate of many other mills through fire in 1802 and 1811, and it was completely gutted in 1871, a fairly common hazard of early cloth and woollen mills. The present structure of red and black engineering bricks was designed by James Ferrabee.

Returning to the towpath, the strong current is explained, after a hundred yards, where the Painswick Stream flows in from Stratford Park and the hills above Painswick. The stream previously passed under the canal to join the Frome. T*he stream was probably used to transport goods up to Stratford Mill in small flat bottomed craft and using simple flash weirs to float the vessel up or down.*

Stratford Mill, formerly grist, fulling and gig mills, was one of the first on the Painswick stream to go out of the cloth trade in about 1738. It was rebuilt solely as a corn mill and both steam and water power were used to drive 21 pairs of mill stones. The main mill was gutted by fire in 1908 but the site remained in use until its eventual closure in 1984. It is now occupied by a supermarket.

Gig - A machine for raising the nap on cloth by passing it over rotary cylinders furnished with wire teeth. The Teasel industry formerly served the same purpose.

Grist - included barley, oats as well as corn. All grist to the mill!

The towpath passes through a narrow gateway with a stone lintel, only just wide enough for towing mules and donkeys and the iron rubbing strake and stonework are scarred by countless towing ropes.

Through the gateway was Wallbridge Basin, the termination of the Stroudwater canal, which was infilled in 1954. Follow the arm of the canal curving left, where the imposing stone building, facing out over the infilled basin, was the headquarters of the Stroudwater Canal Company, built in 1795-97.

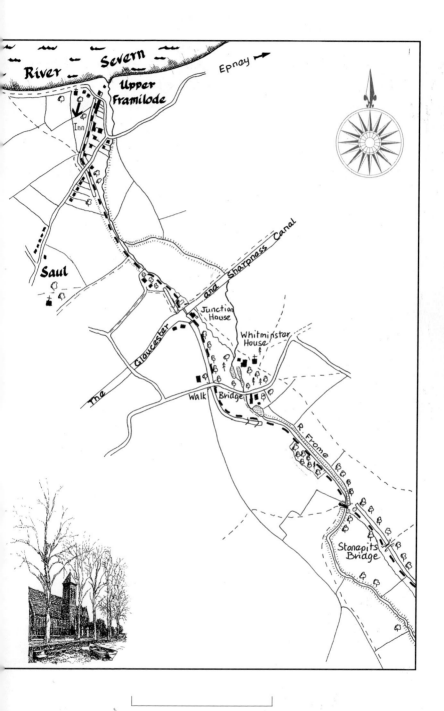

About Half Mile

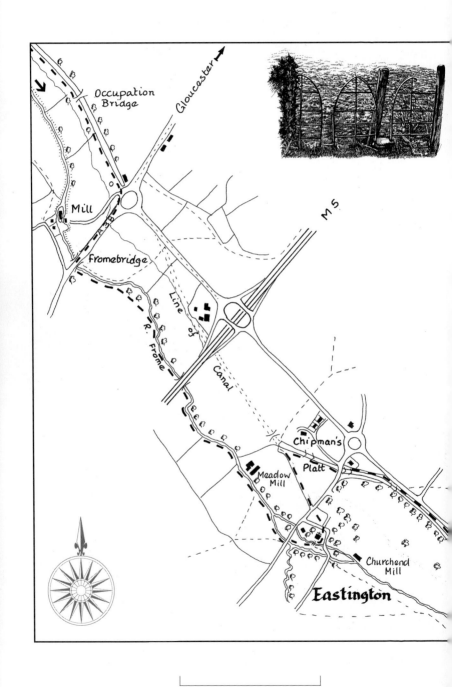

Occupation
Bridge

Gloucester

M.S.

Mill

A38

Fromebridge

Line of

R. Frome

Canal

Chipman's

Platt

Meadow
Mill

Churchend
Mill

Eastington

About Half Mile

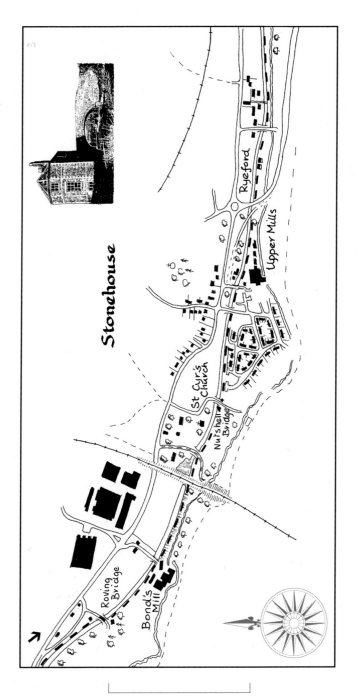

About Half Mile

Crown Copyright MC 100011473

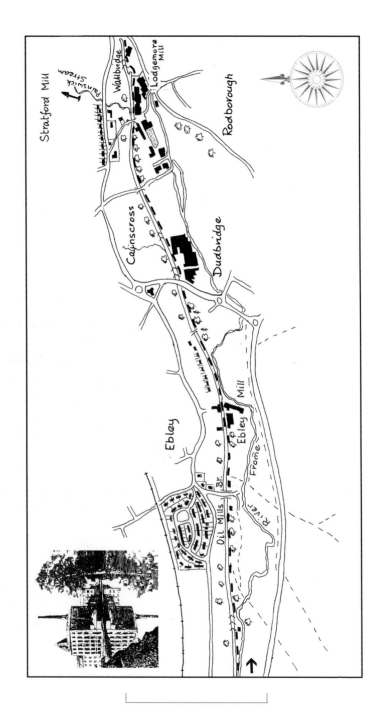

About Half Mile

Stroud and its Woollen Industry

Although apparently not worthy of mention in Domesday Book, *la Strode*, possibly a reference to the marshy confluence of the Frome and the Slad brook, was recorded in 1221 as a settlement within the Hundred of Bisley.

Its position at the meeting point of five valleys meant that the settlement quickly grew in importance, having its own church by 1279 and becoming a Parish in 1304. Gradually increasing commerce resulted in a bridge being erected over the Frome at Wallbridge in 1527, and by 1600 the town had been granted charters for both a market and a fair.

From an early era the production of woollen cloth was carried on along the streams which formed the parish boundaries, but the town also became the commercial and social centre as industry spread along the adjoining valleys.

Mentioned in 1757, as 'a sort of capital of the clothing villages', Stroud became known for high quality, richly-dyed, broadcloth. Scarlet cloth for British Regiments appears to have been a staple of Stroud mills, while Nailsworth and Uley were noted for their blue cloth. A painting in Stroud Museum, showing the canal at Wallbridge in 1785, provides some idea of that industry.

The Frome became commonly known as the Stroudwater and it

seems that the name often designated the whole Stroud valley area and may, occasionally, have been applied to the town.

Flemish weavers are believed to have settled in the area at the instigation of Edward III, but the earliest record of their presence is in 1381. Two Fulling mills were recorded in 1513 and 100 years later eight mills were at work, dominating economic life of the area and providing employment for 19 clothiers, 76 weavers, 33 fullers and 3 dyers.

By 1700 the district was famed for the quality and rich hues of its cloth and the remainder of the century was a period of great prosperity. Clothiers, who were to become well known names, made fortunes, built imposing houses, and generally played leading roles in the industrial development of the Frome valley.

The early 19th century was a period of fluctuation but the population census of 1821 shows, that in Stroud Parish alone, there were 149 weavers, the majority of whom worked looms in their cramped cottages, 32 clothiers, 32 dyers, and 36 shearmen. A further 86 workers were employed in processes which included 'scribblers', 'spoolers', 'spinners', 'burlers', 'pickers', 'rowers' and 'scourers'.

During periods of severe economic slump in the industry a great deal of poverty was caused which was only partly alleviated by charitable enterprise.

The arrival of steam power resulted in many of these processes being mechanised when many mills were enlarged to house new machinery and methods. Almost all of the surviving mill buildings along the Frome and Stroud valleys date from that era. With the introduction of power looms weaving was also brought into the mills increasing production but causing considerable hardship and strife among the weavers and other workers.

The disparity between conspicuous wealth and this deprivation resulted in a considerable rise in crime, particularly of the theft of woollen goods in the course of manufacture, as men, women and children were sometimes made desperate by starvation.

Notes and Recollections of Stroud was published in 1871, and local worthy and amateur historian Paul Hawkins Fisher records many interesting facts and features of everyday life in Stroud up to that time.

He relates, for instance, that between 1801 and 1833, a sum of £520, which had accumulated from penalties inflicted for embezzlement (then the term for stealing from an employer), of materials during manufacture - such as wool, yarn, cloth etc. - was devoted to relieve local poverty. He describes a vivid picture of the times -

'*The embezzlement of clothing materials themselves were called 'slinge'. This offence was very prevalent...for then most of the manufacturing operations were done in the houses of the operatives, to whom wool and yarn was entrusted for carding, spinning, weaving etc...*

Also in the mills themselves great facilities were afforded for secreting, purloining and withholding parts of these materials...and by which the clothiers suffered great losses.

The number of embezzlers and dealers in 'slinge' was also great: with ready purchasers in the numerous small clothiers then still existing, who worked up the 'slinge' with new materials into inferior cloth. At that time stealthy figures might be met in the twilight, crossing Hampton Common from valley to valley; in all parts of the district, from one cottage to another and the lines, or tracks of white stones, which are yet to be seen on the green turf of the common are pointed out as having been dropped there to guide the 'slinge' dealers on their nightly expeditions.

Of these William Niblett was the most notorious...and being a tall, spare man he was popularly called Long Niblett. So large were his transactions that he was once fined £120 as a single penalty. This man was at last found guilty of forgery at Gloucester Assizes and condemned to be hanged But the sentence was commuted to transportation for life on the intercession (it was said) of some Magistrates who thereby purchased Niblett's disclosure of the particulars of his trade, and a large list of his fellow 'slinge-ers', which he gave before he was shipped to Botany Bay.'

The later importance of the Stroudwater canal to the industries of the valleys can be appreciated by descriptions of the local roads at a time when the versatile packhorse was being displaced by increased use of carts and carriages to transport goods in bulk.

Again in *Notes and Recollections of Stroud*, our commentator reveals the old highways to be inadequate and inconvenient for rapidly increasing travel and commerce.

'In olden times, the highway from Stroud to Cirencester and London was up High Street, Silver Street and The Hill to Bisley; thence across Oakridge Common, by way of the dip or hollow called Water-lane, down by Tunley and Henwood, through the river Frome (which is shallow at that place) and the Gulf, to Park Corner; and thence along the whole north side of Oakley Wood and Lord Bathurst's Park, to Cirencester, which it entered at Cicely Hill....

The growing prosperity of Stroud and its neighbourhood required better roads than these; and in the year 1751, parliamentary powers were granted "for repairing the highway from Cirencester to a house called the Blue Boys, near Minchinhampton", and thence over the Hampton and Rodborough Commons down the steep north side of the hill, through the village of Rodborough, and on "to the lower part of Stroud." Also: "for repairing the road from Cirencester toward Bisley as far as the bottom of Gulf Hill," on the Highway before mentioned.

The road to the lower part of Stroud was accordingly repaired, and became a turnpike road; after which, the whole

of that through Bisley was disused as the way from Stroud to Cirencester and London.... [it seems from a clause in the statute that the woolstaplers of Cirencester] ...were desirous of keeping open their communications with the clothing district of Painswick, by way of the old Bisley-road... '
[Probably refers to the old packhorse road from Bulls Cross, through Snows Farm and Piedmont woods to Bisley, followed by the Wysis Way – see end pages].

'*Throughout the whole distance between Stroud and Chalford there are small lateral valleys which break into the main line from both sides, bringing down their tributary rivulets to the Frome at its bottom. And, as all the old highways ran along the sides of the hills, it will be seen that they were rendered difficult and tedious, as well as longer...*

Thus the original road from the lower part of Stroud to Chalford, passed up the town to the end of Lower-street; and then by The Field, until it approached the sharp western edge of the valley of Horns; which caused it to turn down the steep descent to Bowbridge. At this place it turned sharply up the hill to Thrupp, at the farther end of which it passed by the north front of New-house; and, after crossing the two roads from Brimscombe up to Quarhouse and the Lypiatts, it descended into and crossed Toadsmore Bottom, at the Bourne: and thence, passing through Blackness, it entered Chalford in the same direction as doth the present footway.

From what has been said, it will appear that this highway was, through its whole length, very inconvenient both to the clothiers who lived near their mills on the stream, and to the general public who travelled it: in fact, it required a whole day for a team of horses to draw a loaded waggon from Stroud to Chalford, and to return; although the distance [when measured in a straight line along the bottom] is only four miles to the extreme end of the village.'
[All easily followed on Ordnance Survey maps.]

The Golden Valley –
Wallbridge to Sapperton

Wallbridge Lower Lock is the first of 44 locks on the Thames and Severn Canal while the towpath is the beginning of a continuous eight mile walk to Daneway and the Sapperton Tunnel.

The Thames and Severn Canal was built to connect the two great rivers of England, the Severn and Thames. Engineered by Robert Whitworth with 44 locks in the 29 miles between the Stroudwater at Wallbridge and Inglesham lock into the Thames. Opened in 1789, the upper reaches of the canal were never adequately supplied with water which seriously affected the amount of trade and profitability achieved. The section between Inglesham and Chalford was closed in 1927 and the remainder to Stroud in 1933.

Past the lock basin the canal is stopped off by the construction of the latest road system around Stroud centre. Climb the embankment and cross the road to regain the canal side and walk under the Old Bath Road bridge to the steps at the tail of Wallbridge Upper Lock. Restoration of this area carried out by the Canals Trust gives a flavour of what could be achieved over the entire Cotwold canals system.

WALLBRIDGE TO SAPPERTON

The canal widens where Wallbridge wharf, which eventually provided a good source of steady income for the Company, was situated on the far side. But for the next half mile the water is clogged with tangled reeds and fallen trees with the banks close to the water also overgrown.

This length of canal was threatened with extinction in 1988, when the bypass road was planned over the canal bed. But fortune favoured canal preservation and the road took its present line with the canal and towpath re-aligned to the culvert beneath. As the road uses the girder arch in the viaduct originally provided for the canal a new cut will be required through the viaduct in the future.

From the underpass a well used path leads to the viaduct, follow the path forking right under an arch to the road verge. There turn right and take the left of two footpaths down to regain the canal side. It is worth stepping down right, past the stanked off canal, to see the Frome issuing from its culvert beneath the canal bed.

Continue along the towpath, which like the river is now on the left of the canal, past houses on the site of *Arundel Mill, a 17 Century dying mill later used for the manufacture of artificial fertilizer*, and the mill pond. Leaving Stroud behind, the Cotswold scarp appears over the trees in front and the heights of Rodborough stand above the tree covered slopes on the right.

More newish housing is encountered, which seems slightly inappropriate among the remains of old industries and derelict earlier dwellings.

The path narrows as an isthmus between canal and river and then climbs steep steps up to Bow Lane between Stroud and Minchin-hampton. The Britannia Inn is a few yards to the left at the junction with the Cirencester road.

Although the 'bow' has long gone from the present Bowbridge the steps and handrail down the opposite side have the authenticity of the original structure.

From the bridge the towpath narrows alongside more new houses which are not out of keeping for the canal side, and a milestone, its missing plate hopefully preserved somewhere.

The Thames and Severn Canal had milestones erected throughout its length. Cast iron plates were set into the stone showing the miles and half miles going east from Wallbridge while the quarter and three quarter miles were marked from Inglesham westwards. Free standing stones had rounded tops, but where they were set into boundary walls square tops gave better masonry joints.
The plates have mostly disappeared over the years but one or two are preserved or on display in Stroud and Cirencester Museums.

The next stretch of canal has been cleaned and curves right, wide and open, to Stantons Bridge which carries public footpaths in either direction to Thrupp and Butterow, and countryside with sloping fields and trees to the right and a grass bank concealing Griffins Mill to the left.

As the mill building comes into view stone edging along the canal bank indicates the site of the wharf adjacent to the remains of Griffins lock. Next, is the pretty Jubilee Bridge of 1847, which provided access to the mill from the surrounding communities and replaced an earlier bridge, dating from 1742, which had collapsed from neglect - so nothing new there?

Continuing to Ham Mill Lock, where the Bridge has neatly curved abutments and also carries footpath access, followed by a further pleasant open stretch of water. Pink brickwork and aluminium clad industrial buildings border the approach to Bagpath Bridge which is almost a replica of Ham Mills bridge and has been restored by the Canals Trust. A footpath crosses the bridge leading to Thrupp Mill and village.

Hope Mill Lock together with the canal bed has been infilled where it passes industrial premises on the site of *Abdella and Mitchell, a reputable ship building business, which built large steam river launches, both screw and paddle, many of which were for the South American market. The completed vessels passed down the canal and the Severn for shipment from Avonmouth.* The infilling is the worst interruption to restoration since leaving the Severn.

A few yards further along the derelict canal is Gough's Orchard Bridge and Lock but the lock name changed according to who currently owned or worked the adjacent Mill. *A few yards away from this scene of antiquity occasional express trains thunder past creating a strong contrast.*

The infilled canal gives an impression of having been used for cheap and easy rubbish disposal than that of making up sound ground to serve a useful purpose.
Alongside Brimscombe Mill the stone edging indicates the extent of the wharf, and the mill buildings, although of painted brick, still have the appearance of a traditional mill.

The towpath ends as it joins a road close to the Ship Inn, the only survivor of three pubs which once quenched the thirst of trowmen, bargees and canal workers at Brimscombe Port. It will probably also suffice for canal walkers.

The Port was the headquarters of the Thames and Severn Company staffed by clerks, wharfmen, craftsmen, apprentices and labourers. Here goods were transhipped from the seagoing

Trows of the Stroudwater to the narrower Thames barges which only could be accommodated in the locks up and over the canal summit.

The main warehouse and offices, of three stories, were on the wharf at the north side of the basin with a forge and a boat weighing dock. The basin was 700 feet in length and 250 feet wide with a central island for stocking coal and other goods attractive to thieves.

This scene has largely disappeared the Port having been infilled and many of the old buildings removed. Road widening and new buildings now tend to confuse the orientation of the old waterways and buildings of the old Port.

However, from the Ship Inn cross both the road and the Frome to a signed footpath approximating to the canal line. Climb steps up to the roadside and turn right for 100 yards to another footpath, signposted back through the present complex, to Port Mill. The old mill building, together with ancillary buildings, has been renovated and preserved while the adjacent Frome is controlled by weirs and sluices. A plaque on a wall nearby commemorates the site of Brimscombe Port.

Port Mill was known as Fields Mill in the 17th century, when it was used for fulling. Its later name stems from its proximity to the port, and mostly rebuilt, it was later occupied by various cloth manufacturers.

From the Mill follow a narrow access road alongside the Frome and the hidden railway to rejoin the canal towpath where it reverts to vernacular canalside scene at a small access bridge adjacent to Bourne Lock. From the lock basin the canal is restricted to a culvert through the railway embankment while a tunnel provides for the towpath.

WALLBRIDGE TO SAPPERTON

The towpath continues between the canal bed and river while the railway is up on the left above the site of Bourne boatyard. The buildings on the right of the towpath stand on the site of Dark Mills and the canal curves left to Bourne Bridge, where Brimscombe Gas Works once stood.

During the 16th century two fulling and two grist mills occupied the Dark Mill site. In the next two hundred years the mill housed various manufactories including shear grinding and cloth dying, saw milling and umbrella stick manufacture, the last being a speciality of the Stroud area. The mill was demolished in 1964.

Bourne Mills had a succession of uses including fulling, rug making, corn milling and woollen cloth manufacture. In 1822 it combined both the latter and was powered by two water wheels. By 1860 it was used for mattress wool and shoddy manufacture, followed by wood working and then umbrella and walking stick manufacture up to the 1960s.

Another pleasant section of canal leads to the agreeable structure of Beales Bridge and accompanying lock. Iron strakes set in the bridge parapet and the stone work are heavily grooved from years of abrasion by towing ropes.

Visible on the nearby main road is the King and Castle, formerly the Victoria Inn, close to the site of Brimscombe Railway Station. Small sturdy 'tank' engines were kept at the sidings for the purpose of assisting heavily laden trains on the long pull up to Sapperton. As they were regularly needed to refill with water this section of canal had to be kept topped up especially for this purpose. (Which conjures up a fairly nostalgic scene of steam locomotives and horse drawn barges proceeding side by side up the Golden Valley - see Epilogue)

The towpath passes beneath a fringe of chestnut trees through a parkland setting alongside a cleared length of canal where the water is wide and full. As the valley narrows a history of commerce and transportation is defined by the turnpike road high up the valleyside, the railway lower, while the canal contours a few feet above the Frome in the valley bottom.

Another milepost, minus plate, is passed as St Mary's Mill, an attractive group of Cotswold stone buildings, comes into view on the right. St Mary's bridge provides arches for both river and canal and immediately beyond is the lock basin. The skew bridge carrying the railway across again has been infilled to the detriment of the lock.

At the approach to Clayfield's Mill, now renovated as private dwellings, beech saplings are growing along the edge of the towpath and the far bank has been landscaped as a garden area. The pleasant scene is enhanced by Iles's (or Grist's) Bridge and lock basin. A sidestream, which powered the Mill flows into the canal and a sluice under the towpath takes the overflow to the Frome.

Steps lead up from the towpath to a verge where road widening has obliterated the canal bed, and on the far side the site of Ballinger's lock is occupied by a row of lockup garages. This is followed, ironically enough, by a pleasant stretch of canal and bank, leading to Chalford wharf, and the first Round House is encountered alongside the renovated buildings of Belvedere Mill.

Belvedere Mill, alternatively known as Tayloes and Corpus Christi Mill, occupies one of the oldest mill sites in the Chalford valley. Early in its life it was both a corn and fulling mill, and from the 16th century it was a cloth mill . By the mid-19th century it was a corn mill and also utilised for silk throwing. Much of the present building dating from the turn of the 19th century.

The wharf is a pleasant picnic spot still with old sluice gear and moorings. Across the road from the Round House is 'Chalford Place' which was once the *Company's Arms Inn*.

Roundhouses are unique to the Thames and Severn, and five were built, at Chalford, Coates, Cerney Wick, Marston Meysey and Inglesham, providing accommodation for lengthsmen. They consisted of three stories connected by a curving stairway built into the walls, the ground floor being stables and the first and second were living accommodation. Two had convex roofs, as here, while three, at locations where fresh water was not easily available, had inverted roofs to collect rainwater.

The towpath continues past a pair of cottages standing end on to the canal and on the gable wall alongside the path a faintly discernible advertisement reads - *'James Smart - Coal Stone & Sand Merchant...Dealer in Staffordshire Bricks ....'* which seems worthy of preservation?

The canal bed is infilled where a hump backed bridge and Chapel Lock, once stood. Named for the Chapel of Ease, now a Church across the road.

Follow the grass verge for a few yards, passing behind a bus shelter, to regain the canal and towpath. The high stone wall is the boundary of the once extensive Bliss' Mills site now a complex of light industries.

From the 1850's the mill was the centre of a large scale walking and umbrella stick industry, which eventually occupied four mills and became one of the biggest manufactories in the country.

The canal has been encroached by road widening as far as Chalford

Chairs, which is a reasonably appropriate industry for the site of a former woodworking mill.

Cross the Cirencester road where it commences the steep climb up Cowcombe Hill at the site of Bell Bridge. Erected in 1815 to carry the new turnpike road over the canal, Bell Bridge was in turn demolished for the present road layout. The canal is culverted under the road, with the River Frome even lower beneath the canal bed.

Passing Bell Lock chamber, Chalford Railway Station was behind the high retaining wall on the far side. Both Bell Lock and the following Red Lion Lock were named for nearby pubs, of which the Red Lion still exists and can be visited via a convenient footbridge.

> *The completion of Red Lion lock was a landmark for the Canal Company as copious   springs nearby, known as the 'Black Gutter', were available and provided enough water for the canal down to Stroud to be in use long before the rest of the canal was open.*
>
> *Clowse Bridge commemorates this event and is particularly well designed as a memorial to Josiah Clowes, the Company's 'Surveyor, Engineer and Head Carpenter' who supervised the construction of the canal from start to finish.*

The line of the canal changes course where the mill pond of Innell's (or Sevill's), Silk Mill had to be avoided. Off to the right a half height viaduct carries the railway along the edge of this narrow valley.

Around a bend the concrete bridge structure replaces an earlier timber bridge which carried the side road past a former mill house which became the Clothier's Arms, and later, the Valley Inn.

Valley Lock, which together with Bell and Red Lion Locks raised the water level 26' in half a mile, effectively marks the end of Chalford. From here canal and river proceed side by side in an enjoyable rural setting between the wooded valley sides.

After the derelict Chalford Water Works and a further milestone, the towpath becomes an isthmus again between the two waterways, a congenial setting beneath the trees probably little changed since the canals first operated.

A house across quiet fields on the left was *Ashmead's Silk Mill, part of an industry which grew up in the wake of the declining fortunes of the woollen industry.*

The valley opens slightly approaching Bakers Mill Lower and Upper Locks where the road bridge links the villages of Oakridge and Frampton Mansell, both of which have pubs. Just beyond is a footbridge across the canal giving access to the villages, and the Wysis Way, descending from Oakridge Lynch joins the canal towpath.

The Wysis Way links the Offa's Dyke Path at Monmouth to the Thames Path. Crossing the northern part of the Forest of Dean to the Severn at Gloucester before climbing the Cotswold scarp to Bisley and then descending to the valley of the Frome near Baker's Mill to continue with the canal to Thameshead.

The lake above the former Mill was excavated to hold a head of water for the operation of the lower locks.
The juxtaposition of river, canal and railway is a feature of the narrow valley and the viaduct carrying Brunel's Great Western Railway from Swindon is soon in view across the canal.

The towpath continues along a scenic length of canal to Pucks Mill where it crosses to the other side. From the bridge footpaths lead, in a quarter of a mile, to the Crown Inn at Frampton Mansell.

The towpath next passes under Whitehall Bridge, where footpaths lead into Siccaridge and Sapperton Woods, both areas of the Gloucestershire Wildlife Trust. After Whitehall Lower and Upper Locks the towpath reverts to the left bank via a footbridge and, approaching the head of the valley, the locks become more numerous.

Bathurst Meadow is followed by Siccaridge Wood Lower, Middle, and Upper, Daneway Basin and Daneway summit lock - now part of the pub carpark. Some of these higher locks had side ponds, the outlines still partly visible at times, to conserve water in their operation.

During the construction of the canal, the Daneway Inn was the Bricklayers Arms and the centre of activity. This was particularly so when the canal was completed up to that point. As the tunnel was still under construction, goods had to be transferred from the canal barges for road carriage to Cirencester, Lechlade and beyond.

Work continued on the tunnel for a further three years, which probably accounted for the comment that "tunnelling wrote indelible lines of worry on many an engineers face."

Leave the Daneway, perhaps refreshed, and continue along the towpath for half a mile. Just before the canal turns abruptly from the valley in to the hillside it crosses the culvert carrying the Frome. *The river has accompanied the Cotswold Canals Walk, rising 310 feet, from Framilode, and now seeks its own source in the hills to the north.*

WALLBRIDGE TO SAPPERTON

Follow the footpath climbing behind the tunnel portal to a stile, and walk diagonally up the field towards Sapperton Church. From a stile at the top of the field an enclosed track leads to Church Lane, turn right to reach the village street near the school.

> *When twice a hundred years have gone*
> *Across my Cotswold eaves,*
> *And still the woods of Sapperton*
> *Make summer of green leaves,*
> *Come then and sing what song you will,*
> *You lovers of new time,*
> *But sometimes on my Cotswold hill*
> *Renew my Cotswold rhyme.*
>
> 'Legacy'   John Drinkwater

'Saperton' - place of soap makers - probably refers to Fullers Earth found in the vicinity and used in the treading "walking" of the woollen cloth.

Pinsbury Park across the valley, was the home of Sir Robert Atkyns, who compiled a comprehensive 'Doomsday' history of Gloucestershire. His effigy can be found in the church. The poet laureate John Masefield also lived for a time at Pinsbury Park, as did later some of the founders of the Guild of Craftsmen in the county.

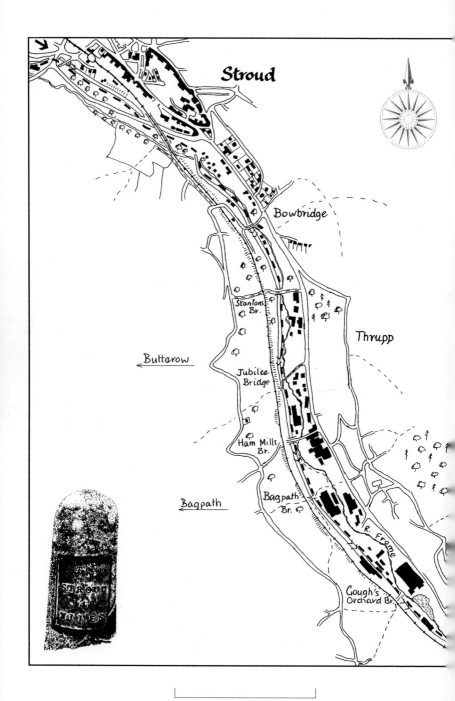

Stroud

Bowbridge

Stanfons Br.

Thrupp

Buttarow

Jubilee Bridge

Ham Mills Br.

Bagpath

Bagpath Br.

R. Frome

Gough's Orchard Br.

STROUD MILES

About Half Mile

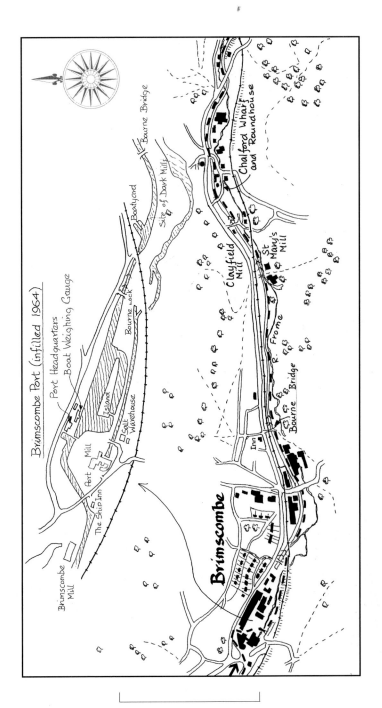

Brimscombe Port (infilled 1964)

Port Headquarters
Boat Weighing Gauge

Bourne Bridge

Site of Dark Mill

Boatyard

Bourne Lock

Island

Salt Warehouse

Port Mill

The Ship Inn

Brimscombe Mill

Chalford Wharf and Roundhouse

Clayfield Mill

St Mary's Mill

R. Frome

Bourne Bridge

Inn

Brimscombe

About Half Mile

Crown Copyright MC 100011473

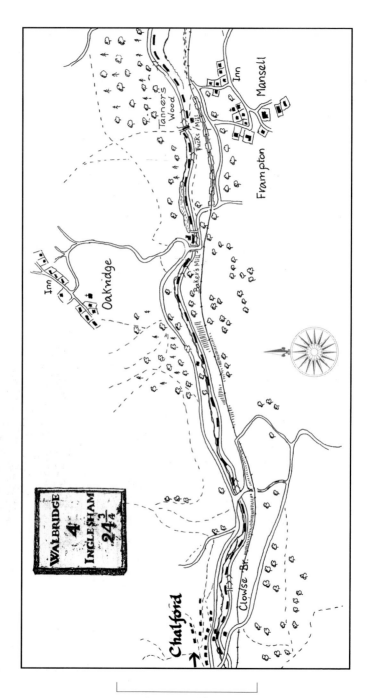

About Half Mile

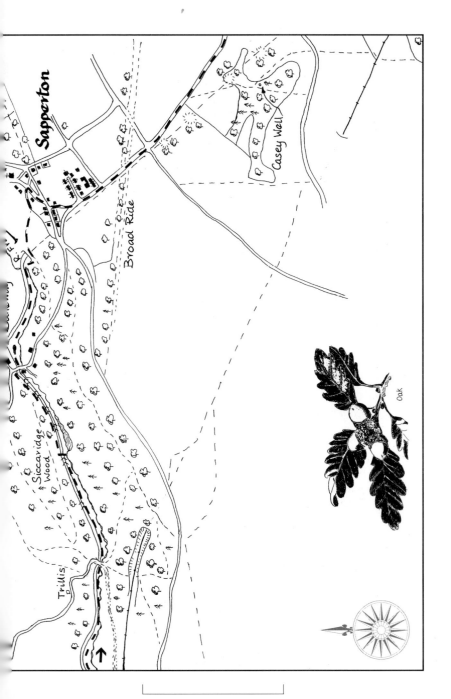

Sapperton

Broad Ride

Casey Well

Siccaridge Wood

Trillis

Oak

About Half Mile

The Summit Waters –
Sapperton to Upper Siddington

From the school cross the road to an alley path opposite and follow this up to join a road.

For the first half mile, the road approximates to the line of the Sapperton Tunnel and tree-clad mounds show the line of some of the twenty five ventilation shafts which were necessary when the canal was constructed. Note that the trees were not originally planted with the environment in mind, but rather as a cash crop on Canal Company land.

After a short distance the road crosses the Broad Ride, one of ten similar which radiate from Oakley Wood, in Cirencester Park, and continue over a crossroad.

As the canal is underground a choice of routes can be taken to the Tunnel House portal, both are pleasant and maintain some interest with the canal.

The first choice comes in about 300 yards after the crossroad, where a footpath leaves the road through a gate on the right. Cross the field angling away from the road and keeping right of the tree covered mound marking a ventilation shaft. At the woodland turn right down a hollow way and through a wicket gate alongside a horse jump. About 50 yards further, at a path junction, is the stone parapet around Casey Well where strong springs caused problems for the tunnel engineers 200 feet below ground, and continue to do so.

Take the left fork and continue downhill and then along a narrow valley which curves right to join the Stroud-Cirencester road. A footpath directly opposite leads to an underpass in the railway embankment and then crosses a field to the woodedge and a hunt gate into Hailey Wood. Follow a path to the right to the The Star from where one of many permissive ways can be followed to the Tunnel House Inn and the canal again.

Otherwise, continue with the Wysis Way along the road for another half mile, to a squeeze stile in the wall on the right. Cross the field to the Stroud - Cirencester road, where a footpath directly opposite leads to a hunt gate and a track into Hailey Wood. The woodland track parallels the canal tunnel in places and the airshafts can be seen on the right, surrounded by deer fences. They should not be investigated.
After 200 yards continue over a cross track, and after 100 yards, cross another of the avenues radiating from Cirencester Park.

The track curves left, descending over a cross track and joining another from the left. Continue, still descending, over a further track, to join yet another track from the left. This curves right through an arch under the railway. Turn left, following the embankment, and shortly reach the Tunnel House Inn.
Now a country pub, it was built solely to cater for the navvies engaged in building the canal tunnel. After a fire 50 years ago it was rebuilt without a third floor which had provided the accommodation for them.

THE COTSWOLDS CANAL WALK

From the Inn walk down to the eastern portal of the tunnel and follow the towpath, still shared with the Wysis Way. The re-building of the eastern portal of the tunnel was one of the first acts of the Canal Trust and most of the original stone was recovered from the canal bed. Currently, trips are available for about a mile into the tunnel but roof collapse, perhaps partly caused by Casey Well, prevents further entry.

Together with the portal, this stretch of canal, named "Kings Reach" after a Royal visit in 1788, remains a showpiece. The next mile along the summit level, although still derelict, exhibits further interest. After the attractive Tarlton road bridge, in half a mile, is Coates Roundhouse, the second encountered so far, standing in isolation. Shortly afterwards is a railway bridge, remarkable for the engineering skill of the skewed brickwork across the canal, and lastly, Coatesfield Occupation bridge.

From the bridge the canal executes a sharp turn and barge towropes have worn deep grooves in the rubbing stones of the arch. Although the canal continues through an ancient site, occupied by our ancestors for centuries, the towpath is no longer a right of way and we are obliged to desert the canal for other public ways.

> *I own all this. Not loutish acres*
> *That tax the spirit, but the hawking*
> *Eye's freehold, paper country.*

> *Thirty two inches of aqueduct*
> *Windmill (disused), club house, embankment,*
> *Public conveniences*

> *In rural areas. This is my*
> *Landlocked landscape that lives in cipher,*
> *And is truer than walking.*

SAPPERTON TO UPPER SIDDINGTON

Red and imperial, the Romans
Stride eastward. Mysterious, yellow,
The Salt Way halts and is gone.

Here, bigger than the hamlets they are,
Wild wayside syllables stand blooming:
Filkins, Lechlade, Broughton Poggs.

Here only I discard the umber
Reticulations of sad cities,
The pull and drag of mud.
    'On Buying OS Sheet 163' U A Fanthorpe

Turn right off the bridge and follow a track which parallels the canal initially. Pass below Tarlton field barn, on the hill to the right, and walk through a gateway and along the edge of the wood to alight, suddenly, at the highest source of the Thames or Isis.

The commemorative stone, erected by the Thames Conservators, replaces a reclining figure, representing either Neptune or Old Father Thames, which graced this isolated spot. It is now at St Johns Lock, Lechlade, presumably because it is more for car borne tourists there. In recent years the water table has lowered dramatically leaving the spring almost permanently dry.

The rivers of Cotswold (with one exception), the Coln, Churn,
Windrush, Evenlode, Leach and lesser tributaries, flow east to
the Thames. The true source is often disputed, but this stream,
from Trewsbury Mead to the Keynes villages and Lechlade, has
been called Isis or Thames for hundreds of years. Springs were
once plentiful in the vicinity but, as elsewhere in recent years,
the water table has become much lower.
The Isbourne, rising on the water-shed above Winchcombe
contrarily flows north into Shakespeare's Avon.

THE COTSWOLDS CANAL WALK

> The Thames Path National Trail meanders for 180 miles from the source to the Thames Barrier at Greenwich.

Now with the Thames Path walk across fields with gates and stiles. From the second gate a path leads uphill to the right, in half a mile, to the Thameshead Inn, built by the Railway Company as the Great Western Hotel, from where the walk can be resumed.

Continue following the boundary of a long field to the Fosse Way, between Tetbury and Cirencester. The canal bed contours the valley on the left where Thames Head Wharf stood adjacent to the road.

Cross the Fosse Way to a stone slab stile and descend steps alongside a culvert which provides, on occasions, for the flow of the infant Thames. Follow the valley bottom for a short distance to the line of a watercourse just below a house which is partly hidden in trees on the line of the canal.

The site of Thameshead Pumping Station, where, virtually throughout the life of the canal, water was pumped from a 64 ft deep well in the effort to keep a sufficient head of water in the canal. A succession of pumping engines were used until a second hand Cornish engine was installed in 1854. This increased the pumping capacity to three million gallons a day. The well never ran dry, demonstrating that although you may not be able to see the Thames, it is, nonetheless, present.

The public footpath now slants up, right, to follow the boundary hedge to a gate. The path then angles down to the river but most walkers will probably be unable to resist walking directly down for their first sight of the Thames, emerging from the limestone on its long meander to Greenwich.

Just before reaching the road, a footpath leads off to the right, which the Wysis Way follows, to Kemble Railway Station and, nearby, the village post office and shop.

Continue across the road following the Thames Path and the stream meandering through fields to reach a small road leading into Ewen. Cross diagonally left to a footpath alongside the stream and pleasantly separated from passing traffic.

Where this path rejoins the road continue for about 350 yards where the Thames Path follows a road to the right. Continue to the next junction and turn left towards Siddington. To visit the Wild Duck Inn continue along the village street for a further 250 yards.

At a fork keep left and continue for about half a mile to a bridge carrying the disused railway over the road. Just prior to the bridge a track on the right leads to Ewen Wharf site, which, together with Halfway Bridge (midway between Wallbridge and Inglesham), has been renovated by the Canals Trust.

The towpath, courtesy of the landowner, twists and dips between trees along this derelict but pleasantly pastoral section to Park Leaze Bridge which is now flat and featureless. The next length of canal has a good water level in winter and a well used path continues for about three hundred yards, where the road must be regained.

Regrettably the canal has been infilled for the next one and a half miles and is inaccessible for most of that distance and another half a mile after that.

Walk along the road, which parallels the line of the canal, for a quarter of a mile, to a footpath over a stile on the left. Furzenleaze Bridge which once crossed the canal here, was sometimes referred to as Level Bridge because the canal was in a cutting rendering the usual hump back bridge unnecessary. The footpath approximates to the towpath alongside the shallow depression of the canal to the site of Bluehouse Bridge, where only the Lengthman's cottage survives.

The track is a public way and turning left for a few paces allows a view of the canal bed landscaped through the garden. Turn about and walk down the track to the road again, turn left for fifty yards to a footpath through a gate on the right which follows the course of a stream. As the stream curves right the foot path turns slightly left up hill to a fieldgate at a road junction.

Before continuing straight across along Clark's Lane, it is worth turning left for 50 yards up to the brow where the line of the canal crosses the site of Minety Bridge. The canal line curves boldly around the countour from Bluehouse to the road and continues in a cutting, overgrown with trees and bushes, towards Upper Siddington.

Resuming along Clark's Lane, round a bend and turn left at a junction to shortly arrive on the canal bridge at Siddington Lock flight.

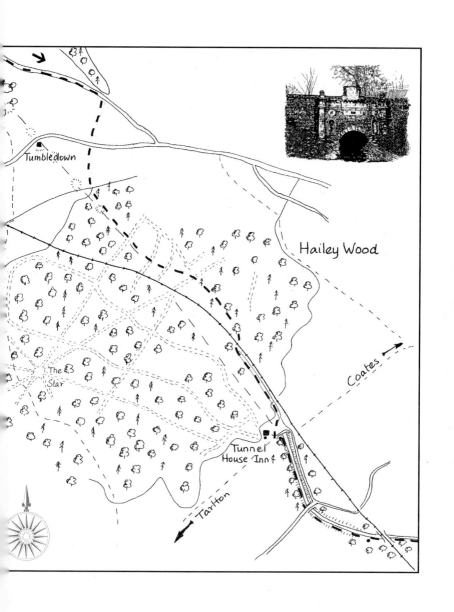

Tumbledown

Hailey Wood

Coates

The Star

Tunnel House Inn

Tarlton

About Half Mile

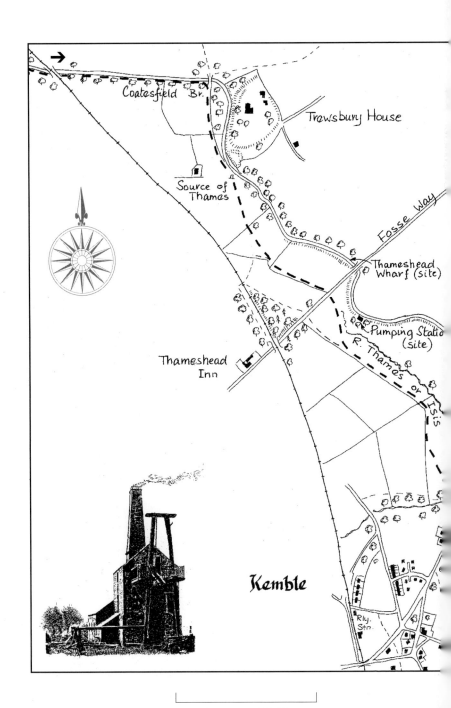

Coatesfield Br.

Trewsbury House

Source of Thames

Fosse Way

Thameshead Wharf (site)

Pumping Station (site)

R. Thames or Isis

Thameshead Inn

Kemble

Rly. Stn.

About Half Mile

Crown Copyright MC 100011473

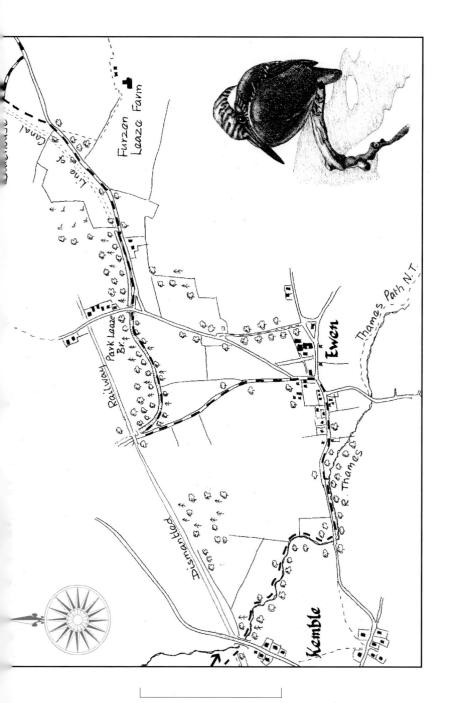

About Half Mile

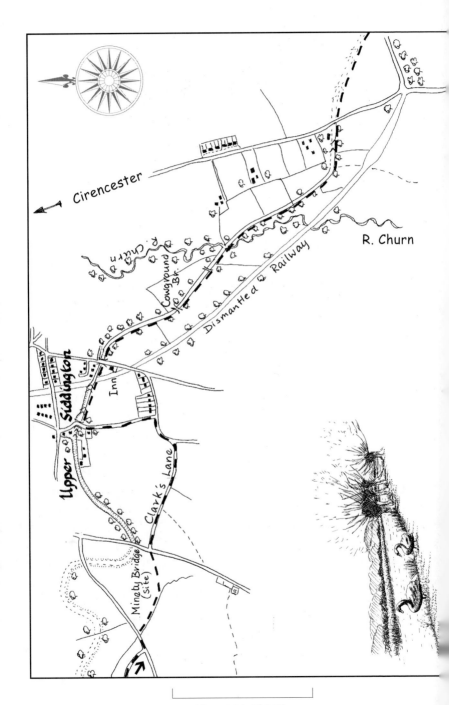

Cirencester

R. Churn

R. Churn

Cowground Bk.

Dismantled Railway

Upper Siddington

Inn

Clark's Lane

Minety Bridge (Site)

About Half Mile

Siddington Flight

Descent to the Thames –
Siddington to Marston Meysey

The Upper Lock, seen over the left parapet, is the first since Daneway Basin and marks the descent from the summit level to the Thames. The bridge provides a good viewing platform down the lock flight over the remains of Second and Third.

A public footpath, presently overgrown, gives access to Upper Lock and the junction Basin where an arm of the canal branched off to Cirencester. The house overlooking the basin was the residence of the Canal Company's Agent and workshops for the eastern half of the canal were also here.

Footpaths and then roads through Love Lane industrial estate (one named for the Thames and Severn engineer Robert Whitworth), can be followed for one and half miles into Cirencester on the approximate line of the canal branch, but few traces remain to be seen.

Walking down the flight it can be appreciated how the combined locks lowered the water 39' from the summit level. Past the remnants of the railway bridge the towpath is channelled narrowly between houses, one of which, built on the site of Lower Lock, is another problem facing restoration.

At the road the Greyhound Inn, a few yards right, is available for refreshment as it was for the boatmen after working their barges down the four locks.

A pleasant and well maintained towpath follows for the next one and a half miles. Much of this was impenetrable blackthorn ten years ago when I had the pleasure of organising the opening up of this length, and greater satisfaction now from the amount of use it obviously gets. The canal bed along this length should be comparatively easy to restore.

Cowground Bridge, one of the few remaining hump backs along the eastern side of the summit, has been renovated by the Canal Trust. The next structure reached is now a utilitarian farm crossing but still has the abutments of the original swing bridge.

A few yards further the towpath crosses the River Churn by a timber footbridge erected when the towpath was cleared by the County Council. Originally an aqueduct carried both canal and towpath over the river which meanders through ancient water meadows here.

Floating Meadows
Improvements to agriculture of the 17th & 18th Centuries included a method where waterlogged rushy meadows could be converted to productive grazing.
A form of irrigation, known as 'floating' was devised so that riverborne nutrients were deposited onto the grassland which, at the same time, was protected against severe winter weather. A controlled depth, no more that an inch, was necessary and the water had to flow constantly otherwise the grass would die.
A highly sophisticated form of drainage divided the land into shallow ridges and furrows, sometimes a hundred yards long

and about ten yards apart. Gutters were cut along the ridges and water reached them via feeders from the nearby river. A feeder might serve up to a dozen ridges, and in very flat water meadows could be a mile long. Sluices carefully balanced, allowed water to spill from the ridge and flow across the slope into the furrow bottom, from where it was directed back to the river.

Great accuracy was needed in setting out the ridges and furrows to ensure that the water flow was maintained at one inch depth. Complex waterways and sluices were required, and often a feeder to one part of the meadow passed over the drain from another. The need for constant maintenance of the system, coupled with the introduction of artificial fertilisers, brought about the end of the practice.

The luxuriant grass which resulted from this practice was reflected in the improved growth of cattle grazing the land after floating. But taking water from the river for this purpose was in direct competition with the long established rights of millers which resulted in disputes and occasional skirmishes when the irrigation channels were destroyed.

In 1790 the return on 1000 acres of improved grassland was claimed to be five times greater than that of all ten mills in the vicinity.

Some features of floating, timber sluices, aqueducts and channels, may still be seen in meadows around Cirencester, some remains being visible alongside the Churn where it crosses the canal.

The next feature along this length is Claymeadow Cutting. It was probably a good source of 'puddling' material for the canal and also resulted in a brickworks being established on the opposite side. The bricks would have been some of the cargo loaded at South Cerney Wharf which stood adjacent to the Lock now landscaped as part of the garden of the former Lock House.

Cross the South Cerney - Cirencester road to a footpath on the line of the former towpath. Undulations in the field mark the outlines of Middle and Lower Locks, which together lowered the canal another 30'.

Cross Northmoor Lane and continue on the towpath. In a short distance a footpath on the right can be followed for a quarter of a mile into South Cerney if required.

Although overgrown and silted the canal bed is wide between the banks as it curves left through open countryside and under willows and a massive oak tree standing in a pollarded coppice, which is carpeted by Aconites in February.

Cross Bow Wow Lane at the site of Crane Bridge and continue along a well surfaced track to Boxwell Spring or Shallow Lock. This lock was built because of the necessity to lower the level to that of nearby springs. It falls a mere 3' 6", and other than Dudgrove Lower Lock it is the shallowest on the entire canal.

Past the entrance to Crane Farm the path reverts to a grass surface alongside a hedge and beneath trees. The canal bed in a slight cutting is dry, ironically so, as acres of water come into view, part of the nearby complex of the Cotswold Water Park. This is a pleasant and secluded length and the Churn, only a field away, is a reminder of how pleasant it was to have the Frome accompanying the canal for so many miles.

Rotting timbers of the lower gates are still lying in the water at Wildmoorway Upper Lock and a few yards further on Humpback Bridge is marked by the remains of brick abutments.

The towpath, pleasantly tree lined proceeds to Wildmoorway Lower Lock which, together with the Occupation Bridge, has been recently renovated by the Trust, but the Lock Cottage remains a ruin.

Together the two Wildmoorway locks lowered the level 18' 6"
which required a great deal of water. A Side Pond, recently
excavated by the Trust, was constructed to alleviate the problem
and store water obtained from the Boxwell Springs. The water
problem was so crucial that it warranted the expense of a Lock
Keeper being stationed along this level to monitor water usage
and avoid wastage.

This pastoral reminiscence is all too soon interrupted by the rush of traffic on the busy Spine road. Constructed along previously quiet and winding lanes to facilitate the exploitation of the vast gravel workings hereabouts and to service the Water Park which has evolved subsequently from the disused excavations.

Cross the road, where a Tourist Information Point and public toilets are a few yards to the right, and continue along the towpath with an expanse of water on the right and gravel workings to the left.

Another secluded length follows, the well used towpath overhung by branches and the boundary wall swathed in mosses while the canal bed, partly hidden by thick undergrowth and decaying timber has the appearance of a Cypress swamp. It seems far removed from the rush of nearby traffic and the commercial enterprise of the Water Park.

The Churn becomes part of the scene again for a few yards before departing to meander through the adjacent fields again. Approaching Cerney Wick the path crosses the boundary with Wiltshire which is then never far away for the next mile or two.

The Round House at Cerney Wick, the third visited so far is a private residence. The lock alongside has been renovated by the Canals Trust and is in good condition although the bridge across the tail is now a flat road crossing and the canal culverted beneath.

Cross a road, where the Crown Inn is within sight to the right, and continue along a length of canal yet to be cleared of growth and silt. The towpath is again very pastoral under an avenue of trees. In the adjacent meadows sheep graze beside the Churn.

In this derelict state canal enthusiasts might find these eastern sections slightly tedious, but most walkers will enjoy the path for its own sake and the fact that it follows an old canal, part of our industrial heritage, is a bonus. The possibility that it may one day be operational again gives a great fillip to the imagination and adds considerable interest to the walk.

Latton Basin was the junction of the Thames and Severn and the North Wilts Canal. Both canals and the outline of the basin are now only undulations in the grass. Other evidence of this junction, including the aqueduct which carried the canal over the Churn, has disappeared. Footpaths can be followed along the line of the North Wilts into Cricklade if desired.

Where Weymoor Occupation Bridge crossed the Thames and Severn a surfaced farm road leads on to a high curving bridge over the dual carriageway between Cirencester and Swindon. From this structure the problems for further restoration can be appreciated.

The Thames and Severn has disappeared under the latest improvements to the Roman Ermin Street. This setback is one of several problems which prevent a footpath route closely related to the canal.
Long sections of the canal between Latton and Inglesham have been infilled and returned to agriculture and little of the original towpath remains accessible. Public paths which might be utilised instead are sparse and of the remaining ten miles to Inglesham, barely two miles of the canal line is accessible and these only spasmodically.

As this guide book is intended primarily for walkers rather than pure canal enthusiasts, I have used a route, mainly on field paths, which will satisfy most tastes while retaining a few canal highlights.

The present path system though the parish of Kempsford was a final setback. The OS Explorer map reveals an otherwise adequate network but with several ridiculous anomalies which should have been rectified years ago. Two long paths leading towards Lechlade have missing links rendering them cul de sacs. A third path, also a likely through route, has a middle section which was closed by the Ministry of Defence some years ago, again rendering it inaccessible by the public.

Despite this sorry state of affairs it is fortunate that this crossing of the virtual motorway has been provided, and also that, while the road is private, public bridleway rights exist over it.

Cross the flyover and at Street Farm turn right along the old main road, crossing over to turn into Latton village where the junction is guarded by a mediaeval stone cross.

Walk along Gosditch (Go§d's Ditch) - possibly a medieval boundary which is also found in Ashton Keynes) and continue past the church to a gate way. A bridleway surface exists alongside the deeply rutted farm track and, as it curves left is accompanied by the Ha Ha of the Manor House away on the left. Leave the bridleway at a junction and follow the right hand of the three tracks, which, after half a mile, crosses the Ampney Brook back into Gloucestershire. The County boundary was probably delineated by double gates which exist no longer, while the pillars and plinths are deteriorating rapidly.

Continue along the track to a gate and stile. Cross this and just past the Lodge keep left on a footpath through the trees which soon joins a surfaced road outside Down Ampney church. If you miss the path under the trees turn left in a few yards at the T junction and follow the track to the church.

The village and Church are memorable for several reasons. All Saints was consecrated in 1265, but, as with many other communities, plagues, the Black Death, struck in the Middle-Ages. Aerial photographs show a settlement in the fields near the church and Manor House, which might indicate that villagers abandoned their disease ridden community and moved to the present day village, leaving their church fairly isolated.

The pointed arches between the round Norman pillars have 13th Century decoration of red cinquefoil flowers, which may have been intended to portray the rash which appeared on the skin of unfortunate victims. The individual flower designs may also have been memorials to the villagers who died from the plague. The rhyme, 'Ring a ring of Roses we all fall down', which has endured as a nursery game for centuries, also signifies the floral motif and symptoms of the Black Death.

There are also many reminders in and around the church of Down Ampney's involvement with the invasion of Europe during the Second World War.

A stained glass window commemorates the loss of life associated with the Arnhem Landings, while an Annual Service, together with a small Garden of Remembrance behind the church, serve to commemmorate all involved.

The airfield was built in 1944 in preparation for D Day - the invasion of German occupied Europe. Thirty eight Dakota aircraft and nineteen Gliders were allocated to 271 Squadron stationed here and exercises to perfect the landing of supplies, dropping parachutists and low night flying was practised during May 1944.

Thirty three Dakotas towed Gliders across the Channel during 6th June 1944, and by 20th July, 3000 wounded servicemen had been flown back to England by Air Ambulance Dakotas with nurses on board.

MEMORIES OF DOWN AMPNEY

In a recent Church Newsletter Mrs Freda Hughes, an ex WAAF, records her memories of that momentous time:

'Down Ampney - where's that? Coastal Command say its near Cricklade - so off I went and arrived at Station HQ - a Nissen hut in the middle of a muddy Co-op field - a Wimpey earthmover in the background. WAAF site? 2 miles away - don't worry, we'll issue a bike! A shorthand typist clerk to the CO Group Captain Bradbury. So in February 1944 began the happiest 18 months of my Service life.

A small Cotswold village between Cirencester and Swindon comprising a church (birthplace of Ralph Vaughan Williams), the Home Farm, Herbert's bakery and a few houses. Around this grew an enormous RAF station which was to send gliders full of paratroopers to Normandy on D Day and then for the Dakotas to return with the wounded for initial treatment at a full scale hospital unit.

So many memories - Wimpey cheese sandwiches (4 inches thick) - Herbert's buns (too far to go to the cookhouse) - tea on a boiling ring in an old jam tin in the office!

Flights with G/Capt Bradbury in his own small plane to look at Blakehill Farm and the satellites - the first glider 'snatch' off the airfield - D Day, then Arnhem and the sorrow of losing so many. The good friends made - the RAFDA players - our first effort 'The Dover Road' produced by Ted Howard our Education Officer, furnishing courtesy of Mrs Tucker of Home Farm. So many friends - some still in touch - others alas gone. I count myself lucky to have known them at Down Ampney!'

Continue from the church, and in about 300 yards turn right over a stile. Angle left across an orchard, ignoring another path forking left, to a further stile which exits onto a track, cross over and follow an enclosed track to the village street.

Turn right and after a 100 yards fork right at a junction, following a back road for over a quarter of a mile to a T junction. Continue straight ahead, through a gate, and follow a headland path for three quarters of a mile to Castle Hill Farm. Cross the farm access road, through a gate and continue, now with the hedge on the left, along the edge of two fields.

Entering a third field turn right and gradually converge with the stream in the top left hand corner. Round a bend follow the stream left to a footbridge and cross into Wiltshire again. Walk down the field bearing right of farm buildings, to a handgate, with a signpost alongside, leading onto a track and to the village street in Marston Meysey.

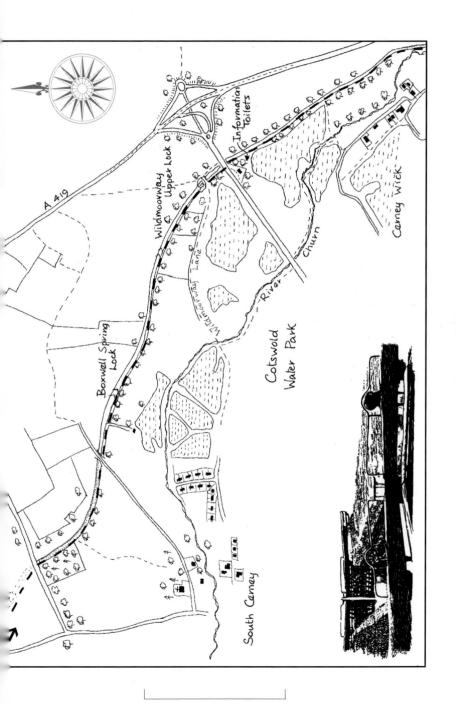

About Half Mile

Crown Copyright MC 100011473

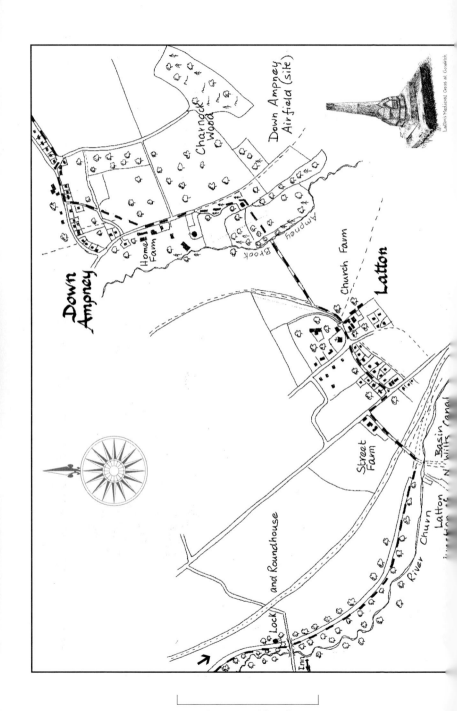

Latton's Medieval Cross at Gosditch

Down Ampney

Charnock Wood

Down Ampney Airfield (site)

Home Farm

Ampney Brook

Church Farm

Latton

Street Farm

Lock and Roundhouse

River Churn

Latton junction & N Wilts canal

Basin

Inn

About Half Mile

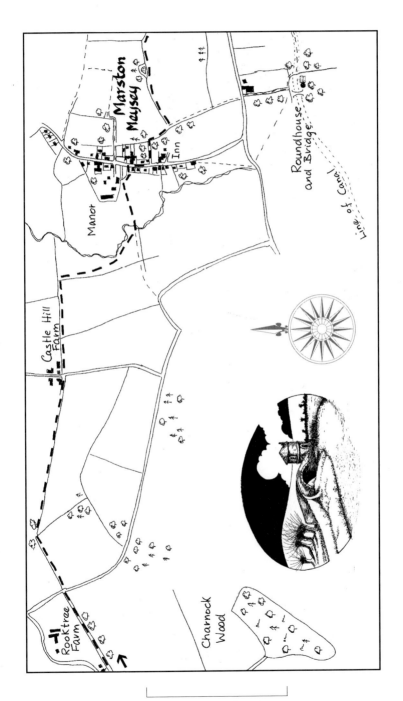

About Half Mile

Crown Copyright MC 100011473

Diversions and Meanders –
Marston Meysey to Lechlade

Turn right along the village street and after 100 yards cross to an unmarked footpath up steps over the remains of a slab stile. For refreshments at the Spotted Cow Inn continue down the street for a further 150 yards. At the end of the enclosed path turn right, now on a bridleway, and at the next field boundary, turn left along the headland.

> *Enthusiasts wishing to see Marston Meysey Round House and the line of the canal should continue, without turning left. At the road cross and continue along the driveway, a public footpath, to the Round House. Only the rendered curve of the tower is visible and the Occupation bridge can be glimpsed, but neither are accessible and high fences prevent further views or photographs from the footpath around the property. A route can then be followed if desired along the infilled canal bed and field paths almost into Castle Eaton. Roads lead back to the main walk near Oatlands Bridge.*

Pass trees on the left concealing a pond, and through a gap in the next boundary continue to a coppice which has been extended over the bridleway. At the end turn right through a gap and then left to continue on the correct line. At the next boundary a ditch and hedge bar progress. Go left through a gateway and immediately right through another, to regain the headland and continue to a hunt gate.

Cross the end of a narrow paddock to a second hunt gate and then follow the hedge on the left for 50 yards to a footbridge. Cross and walk down the headland to reach a narrow lane and turn right to a T junction where Kempsford is to the left. Oatlands Bridge, on the line of the Thames and Severn canal, stands in splendid isolation 200 yards away directly across the road. It can be visited by following the farm track which leads onto the bridge but this is not a public way.

At Kempsford turn right along the village street, under the gaze of four botanic gargoyles in the opposite hedge. The street parallels the line of the canal which runs close behind the Axe and Compass (a navigation inn if ever there was one?)

Continue, passing an old village pump and the remains of the village green to The George Inn. A few yards further, Wharf Lane leads down to the former Wharf House and the line of the canal. Both are in private hands and little can be seen.

Continue down the street to Ham Lane, on the left. A few paces past the turn is the site of Kempsford Bridge with the line of the canal visible on both sides. There is no public access available to the line of the canal continuing towards Inglesham and the Thames.

Turn and walk along Ham Lane which after the last of the bungalows becomes a gravelled track. Step aside at an open gateway on the left where the distinct line of the feeder canal from the River Coln at Whelford is visible inside the hedge.

The Whelford feeder was essential in providing a head of water

83

for the remaining locks at Dudgrove and Inglesham. The water came from the outflow of Whelford Mill, the last on the Coln, and the slight fall available across the flat land between the villages required constant clearance to maintain a flow. The shallow depression of this narrow waterway is obvious in the wide verge of the road between Kempsford and Whelford.

At a junction with Washpool Lane cross and go through the right hand of the two field gates, each with stiles adjacent. Follow the track alongside old gravel workings and then fields which rise slightly on the right. For some odd reason this public path ends abruptly at Ham Barn, an anomaly which also occurs on adjacent paths. Fortunately, by courtesy of local farmer, Mr Bruce Arkell, a permissive route continues.

Fifty yards before the barn turn left across a footbridge and then right, following the stream. After about three quarters of a mile the permissive path links to a public footpath crossing the field from the left.

In a further 200 yards turn right over a concrete access bridge and then left, following the field edge around the angle of woodland which conceals the River Coln. Where the path meets the lane between Whelford and Dudgrove Farm turn left, crossing the river, and after a quarter of a mile, at the end of Bowmoor Plantation, turn right on a track alongside the extensive and attractive Bowmoor Lakes.

The track continues pleasantly, for a mile and three quarters, to a junction, where a footpath straight on leads directly into Lechlade. It is much more preferable to turn right and walk towards the terminus of the Thames and Severn canal.

Inglesham Round House and Occupation Bridge are in private hands and, as at Marston Meysey, inaccessible. Neither the terminal basin nor the site of the lock between the canal and the Thames can be viewed.

Instead turn left to a pretty footbridge across the Thames. Turn left and walk alongside the river to Halfpenny Bridge, where the Canal Company's wharf and warehouse now provide facilities for tourism - and into Lechlade.

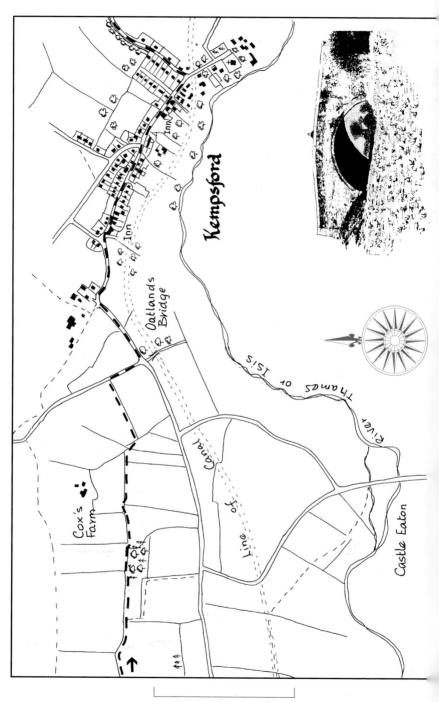

About Half Mile

Crown Copyright MC 100011473

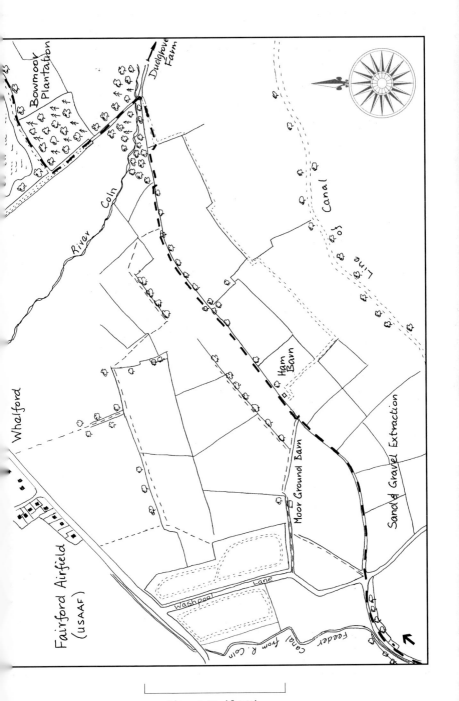

About Half Mile

Crown Copyright MC 100011473

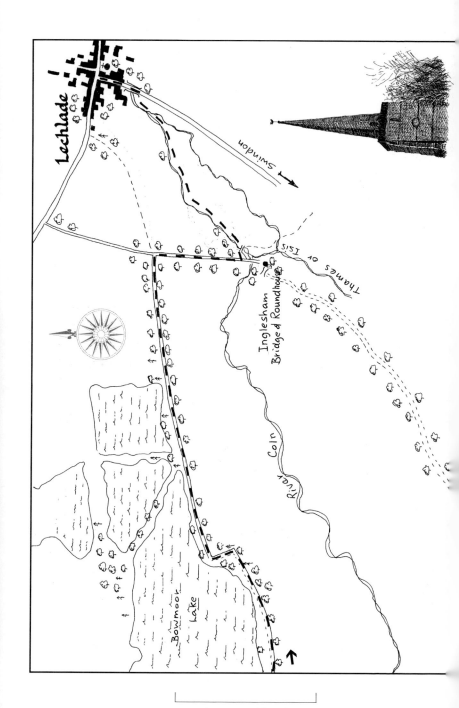

Lechlade

Swindon

Thames or Isis

Inglesham
Bridge & Roundhouse

River Coln

Bowmoor
Lake

About Half Mile

Epilogue

The story poem 'Gloucestershire Exile' has appealed to me ever since I first came across it in *'Cotswold Lad'* many years ago and I have long had a yen to reproduce it in the context of a walk through Gloucestershire. It will no doubt appear old fashioned and antiquated to some eyes, but I think it suits the theme of this walk endeavouring to relate to industry and life along the Stroud and Golden Valley of that time.

Sid Knight's vivid picture of working in and around Brimscombe catches the atmosphere of life when both canals were still operating and goods still occasionally transhipped from Severn trows to Thames barges. His first hand acquaintance of the mills and foundries around Brimscombe, and handling rag-flocks, cases of pins and walking sticks, animates the otherwise mundane recording of such things. His nostalgic record of a part of his life serves equally for the bygone age of the G.W.R.and the canal era.

GLOUCESTERSHIRE EXILE

I was once a porter on the line at Brimscombe up the Stroud
   Valley.
It was just after the first war and jobs were hard to get in 1919.
But the Exchange Clerk said, 'They are signing on
Extra men at Gloucester to meet the 8-hour day and you may
   be lucky.'
So I took the railcar to Cheltenham (change at Malvern Road)
And then the train to Gloucester where

THE COTSWOLDS CANAL WALK

Old Daddy Brewster in uniform frockcoat and gold braid
Looked me up and down and said,
"You don't look strong", and I thought,
Neither would you if you'd had meningitis
At the Crystal Palace, malaria in Freetown and frostbite in
    Vladivostock,
And sailed for four years on salt pork and Fanny Adams.
But I kept my mouth shut as jobs were hard to get in 1919.
Daddy barked: 'Can you load trucks?' and thinking
Of shovelling coal out of the rolling, plunging
Collier's hold at the Abrolhos Rocks in the
South Atlantic and other places, I said,
'Give me a chanGe and I'll show you that I
Can load trucks or anything else', for I did
Not want to go back home without landing
The job as they were hard to get in 1919.
'Tut, tut' said Daddy, 'the war's over now
Me lad but here's your free pass and report at Brimscombe on
    Monday.'
So on a fine spring morning in my thick, coarse
Blue serge with G.W.R. on my cap tally instead of H.M.S.
I landed on the platform at Brimscombe with
My camphor-wood sea chest bought in the
Street of the Sandalwood Makers at Hong Kong,
And wishing myself back in Kowloon on payday
With Hookey the Sparker, Pincher the bunting-tosser,
Nobby the armourer and Bert, cook's mate.
'Are you the new porter?' asked Fatty Peyton,
My God, I thought, you've never been on salt
Pork and Fanny Adams, as I answered 'Yes'.
I didn't know whether to 'sir' the old boy or not.
He said, 'Report to Dan Randle down at the goods
Shed ", as he waddled off to his office, stiff
With gold braid like a Rear Admiral.

Dan, dear old Dan, grinned at me and said, 'What mob?'
I grinned back and said, cocking a chest, 'RN.'
'Goodo', said Dan, 'let's go up to the Vic an'
Have a pint and then we'll fix you up with digs',
But lodgings were as scarce as jobs in 1919,
And we searched all day and drank many pints
Before the widow, Granny Mills, in the little
Thatched cottage up the lane said, 'I'll take
You in if you don't mind sharing a bed with my
Other lodger, and the charge is thirty bob a week in advance'
She made us both a cup of tea, and as the canary
Whistled as the afternoon sun shone in through
The window, I knew that I had found a good home with
    Granny Mills.
'Of course that includes your washing', she said
As we got up to go, So I paid my thirty bob on the spot, and as I
Worked it out this left me with a pound a week for myself,
Which wasn't bad seeing that jobs and digs were both hard to
    get in 1919.
The next day I started work in the yard loading
Trucks with dusty rag flocks, craggy pig iron,
Heavy cases of pins and walking sticks, castings
From the foundry at Ham Mill, and worst of all
They were felling timber at Toadsmoor Lake, and
We had to handwind the big trunks from timber carriage to
    truck,
With the crane, which nearly broke my back,
Still weak from meningitis,
And as I slogged in the rain up to my shoe tops in black slush,
I thought if only I were going ashore in my
Snow-white ducks at Shanghai to see Nelly
The Eurasian dancing girl who lived in the Bubbling Well
    Road.
('Come on sailor, they cried. 'Pull your weight. You're not

aboard ship now.)
But Sunday came at last, and in my new blue pinstripe
And fancy socks (how I fancied myself in my first civvy suit),
I walked out with Dan the checker, dear old Dan,
Chasing the mill girls from Bussage to Bowbridge,
Chalford to Cainscross, the rosy-cheeked dark-eyed
Gloucestershire girls with the husky voices, and
Later on I married one, bless her, in the little stone church at
    Brimscombe up the hill.
But before that came to pass I roamed the green
Hills with Dan, sampling the beer at all the pubs,
And I remember those lovely summer evenings of 1921,
Sitting on the lawn of the Bear of Amberley,
Drinking deep out of tall, blue-black tankards,
Then walking home in the twilight past
Tom Long's Post at the crossroads, and under
The cool, giant Minchinhampton oaks, singing out service
    songs,
Especially the one of Dan's which went:
'Form fours and order arms, and eyes to the rear,
We're the boys that do no work we're always after beer,
We're the heroes of the night and we'd sooner drink than fight,
We're the heroes of the Porters' Fusiliers.
'And Granny Mills said as we rolled home: 'Boys will be boys,'
As she set out my bread and cheese, and watercress
She had gathered from the brook which ran down the bottom
    of the garden.
And then to bed to be awakened in the morning by
The Massed Bands of the Brigade of Blackbirds
In the apple orchard on the bank across the lane,
Where the blossom lay, a foamy, lacy tablecloth on the green
    grass,
Just like the green rollers off the Cape, ruffled by the south-easter.
And now here I am an old man licking my wounds.

And as I look out of the window of this monstrous,
Slab-sided, steel and concrete cliff dwelling in Johannesburg,
All I see are dusty minedumps, rusty corrugated iron roofs,
And one lone peeling blue gum just to remind me that such
    things as trees exist.
And so I shut my eyes to it all, and wish that I
Was once again a porter on the line at Brimscombe up the
    Stroud Valley
Cycling home to tea at five o'clock on a summer afternoon,
With the sun spilling his sundust along the Golden Valley,
From Bussage to Bowbridge, Chalford to Cainscross,
And all around me the lovely Gloucestershire hills.

Mileages

	Miles	Accumulated
Framilode		
Eastington	4.75	4.75
Bridgend	2.5	7.25
Wallbridge	3.25	**10.5**
Bowbridge	1	11.5
Brimscombe	2	13.5
Chalford	1.5	15
Daneway	3.5	18.5
Sapperton	1	**19.5**
Tunnel House	2.75	22.25
Thameshead	1.75	24
Ewen	1.75	25.75
Upper Siddington	4	**29.75**
Cerney Wick	4.75	34.5
Latton	1.25	35.75
Down Ampney	1.25	37
Marston Meysey	2.25	**39.25**
Kempsford	2.25	41.5
Inglesham	4	45.5
Lechlade	1	**46.5**

Tourist Information Centres

GLOUCESTER
28 Southgate Street,
01242 421188

CIRENCESTER
Corn Hall,
Market Place,
01285 654180

SWINDON
37 Regent Street,
01793 530328

STROUD
Subscription Rooms,
George Street,
01453 765768

FARINGDON
7A Market Place,
01367 242191

OXFORD
St Aldates Chambers,
01865 726871

Also by Gerry Stewart:

THREE CHOIRS WAY

A footpath between Gloucester, Hereford and Worcester, with a theme linking the walk and the Music Festival celebrated at the three Cathedrals for over 300 years A glorious walk of 100 miles through the attractive and varied countryside of the three counties, evoked in the old adage "blessed is the eye between Severn and Wye". **Price £5.95**

To obtain any of these books post-free, please send cheque to:

COUNTRYSIDE MATTERS
15 Orchard Road, Alderton
Tewkesbury, GL20 8NS

www.countryside-matters.co.uk

Countryside Matters aims to produce descriptions of pleasant walking, through Gloucestershire and adjoining areas, with strong local connotation and a depth of feeling for the old footpath ways through the countryside.